I Love You Phillip Morris

A True Story of Life, Love, and Prison Breaks

By Steve McVicker

MIRAMAX BOOKS

NEW YORK 2003

FOR INFORMATION ADDRESS:

Hyperion, 77 West 66th Street

New York, New York 10023-6298

ISBN 0-7868-6903-8

10 9 8 7 6 5 4 3 2 1

table of contents

foreword

It's not easy to verify the claims of a con artist. I supposed that's why they call them "artists." Steven Russell is
certainly worthy of the title.

I first met Russell in January 1997, on a bitterly cold
night in Huntsville, Texas. Located about 75 miles north
of Houston, Huntsville is the headquarters for the massive Texas prison system, the nation's second largest, with
almost 150,000 inmates. On that brutal winter evening,
as a Texas blue norther rolled through the town, a few
other journalists and I watched as a team of fugitive trackers
returned Russell to the state prison system's central
intake unit. I had been interested in Russell ever since the

previous summer, when he had authorized his own release from the Harris County Jail in Houston by impersonating a state district judge over the telephone. But as I observed his return to the custody of Texas prison officials—following his then most recent escape, in which he passed himself off as a doctor—it was hard to believe that this pudgy, balding man, shackled at the wrists and ankles, could be the same guy who had been embarrassing state and federal law enforcement officials for years.

Later that night, when Russell was brought before the media for a prison press conference, he had a fresh crewcut, which I thought made him look a little bit more the part of a dangerous criminal. When I finally got the chance to talk with him one on one, I was struck by Russell's charm and friendly eager-to-please manner. He apologized for not responding to a letter I had sent requesting an interview with him several months earlier. It just hadn't fit into his plans, he explained with a wry grin. Indeed, I now knew that, at the time, he had been concentrating on his next escape.

During the next few years, I went on to write several pieces about Steven Russell for the *Houston Press*, the alternative newsweekly I worked for back then. Russell and I stayed in touch through occasional letters. He even called me (collect) from the jail in Broward County, Florida, following his most recent escape from the Texas

Department of Criminal Justice (TDCJ). That time, Russell had managed to evade custody by convincing Texas criminal justice authorities that he was dead.

It was then that I wanted to learn more about his man who seemed as incapable of staying in prison as he did of staying out of it. Maybe I'd even write a book about him. But while Russell could not have been more enthusiastic about the idea, the TDCJ public affairs office did not go out of its way to cooperate. In October 2001, I contacted TDCJ's media office in Huntsville and requested several unfettered interview sessions with Russell. While the initial indication was that there would be no problem granting my request, two months later, despite my follow-up phone calls and emails, I had no further reply from the prison media office. So I switched to plan B: I would wait until after the first of the year to push the issue with TDCJ, and begin my research from the outside.

So, a couple of weeks before Christmas, I traveled to Russell's hometown of Norfolk, Virginia, and to his old haunts in North Carolina, and interviewed as many of his friends and family as possible. Russell's people were hospitable and, for the most part, cooperative. During interviews with a few of his relatives, however, I got the impression from the embarrassed and apprehensive look on their faces that they feared that Russell's troubles somehow suggested evidence of a terrible flaw in the

Russell family's gene pool. Never mind the fact that Russell had been adopted.

After the holidays, I tried again to arrange interviews with Russell through the TDCJ media relations staff in Huntsville. And again nothing happened. At that point, I decided to try going around the Huntsville office, and contacted TDCJ's public affairs division in Austin. Again, officials indicated that my request would be granted. And again, weeks went by with no interview.

Finally, in early February 2002, I received an email from the TDCJ public affairs office in Huntsville stating that I could not have any official "media" visits with Russell, since I was already on his "personal" visitors list. It had taken them four months to either figure that out or to conjure up that excuse. In the past, the current batch of TDCJ public affairs officers had always dealt with me in a fair and straightforward manner. So, this time around, I prefer to think that their hands were tied by officials higher up on the prison system food chain.

So, at that point, I decided to simply start visiting Russell on regular visiting days—either Saturday or Sunday between 8:00 A.M. and 5:00 P.M.—alongside all the countless other people who give up all or part of their weekends to spend a couple of hours in the company of incarcerated loved ones. Over the next nine months, I regularly made the 430-mile round-trip drive from

Houston to the prison facility known as the Michael Unit in Tennessee Colony, Texas, to "visit" with Russell for two hours at a time. We called them our "Saturday brunches." Every visit, I would bring a sack full of quarters and buy Russell as many soft drinks and bags of junk food as he could consume in 120 minutes as we discussed his life. During those sessions, I discovered he has a special affinity for Big Red sodas and Almond Joy candy bars.

We also developed quite a dialogue by mail. At the beginning of the year, Russell purchased a typewriter and I bought him $50 worth of stationery, which Office Depot delivered to him at the prison. Every week, I mailed Russell the questions that I had thought of on my Saturday afternoon drive home to Houston, or the questions I came up with as I wrote. And every week, Russell sent back detailed answers. Thanks to the Department of Criminal Justice's lack of cooperation, I never had the bother of transcribing any of my interviews with Russell. They arrived in my mailbox already transcribed.

As with any journalistic endeavor, I was left with the task of verifying what Russell told me, and wrote in his letters. Most of the conversations recounted in this book are based on his recollections. Unfortunately, many of the people who could have substantiated or disavowed his claims chose not to. Those people include Russell's brother, Scott; his birth mother, Brenda Basham; his late boyfriend James Kemple's mother, Helen; and Victor Rodriguez, the former executive director of the Texas Board of Pardons and Paroles. Nor was Russell's ex-wife, Debbie, especially forthcoming. Likewise, Assistant U.S. Attorney Peter Goldberg said he would agree to an interview if the Department of Justice's public affairs office approved it. Despite my numerous phone calls, representatives of that office never got back to me.

Nonetheless, to my pleasant surprise, during my attempt to confirm Russell's account of his life, I never once caught him in a lie. I'm not saying he never lied to me. But I never caught him lying. Additionally, I am convinced that Russell has an uncanny memory. He claims to have an IQ of 163, and I can certainly believe it's true.

Additionally, I'd like to thank Russell for his patience over the past months. Earlier this year, he sent a letter to my literary agent, Peter Steinberg, asking if Peter had any books he could send him, or if he had any freelance proofreading work Russell could do. Apparently, Russell was getting bored with his surroundings and his keepers.

"The only reason I have remained incarcerated," he wrote matter-of-factly to Steinberg, "is so that Steve can finish his book."

God help the good men and women of the Texas Department of Criminal Justice. They're going to need it.

chapter one

Falling for Phillip Morris

Steven Russell was not looking for love in the law library of the Harris County Jail in Houston when he saw Phillip Morris for the first time. In that dismal place, a cramped, windowless, bunkerlike room with metal folding chairs and tables surrounded by rows of shelves full of ponderous lawbooks, it's hard to imagine the blossoming of any sort of romance.

"It isn't easy for anyone to become intimate with me," says Russell, a chameleon of a man who often alters his appearance depending on his needs. At the time that he met Morris, he was verging on pudgy, with pale skin and dark hair that he combed carefully to try and hide encroaching baldness. "I live in my own little world. I build walls around me to keep from getting hurt. I don't understand why I'm like this. I've never tried to analyze it. It takes a lot of bumps in the road before I am able to trust another person."

As Russell sat in the county jail contemplating his three-year sentence, he had to admit that, for most of the past five years, it seemed his life had been nothing but bumpy.

In fact, despite his current surroundings, Russell had been a model citizen most of his life—at least on the surface. He grew up in comfortable circumstances as the adopted son of a devout, God-fearing couple who owned a prosperous wholesale produce business in Norfolk, Virginia. Like his adoptive parents, Russell, too, was religious. He played the organ—and played it well—on Sundays at church. He married the local police chief's secretary, with whom he fathered a daughter, and even served briefly as a police officer himself in Chesapeake, Virginia, and Boca Raton, Florida. Later, he worked as an executive with food distribution companies in Houston and Los Angeles. He helped federal authorities crack a couple of kickback schemes in the food industry by providing investigators with inside information. He even wore a wire for the feds—twice.

Somewhere along the way, though, Russell had made a conscious decision to turn his back on the law and a life of the status quo. He revealed his homosexuality to his friends and, eventually, his family. He forsook the teachings of his childhood, and embraced a life of crime. It was a life in which he flourished, for the most part. But more than his talents as a thief and a confidence man, it would be the flamboyant, nonviolent brilliance of his jail and prison escapes—usually on a Friday the 13th—that would eventually earn the affable, quick-witted but occasionally vengeful Russell a national reputation in law enforcement and the media. He became known as the King of Con. There was, however, at least one small chink in the legend: Russell sometimes made the mistake of listening to his heart.

Only later would Russell come to see that day in the library as the start of a new phase of his life, rendering him unexpectedly vulnerable. Russell, the ultimate con artist, would become blindly obsessed with one man: Phillip Morris.

In the spring of 1995, in the dull fluorescent light of the Harris County Jail law library, with its dingy walls and desperate patrons, Russell watched Morris with interest. This in itself was not unusual; Russell regularly studied people, looking for habits and potential weaknesses to exploit later. But from his first glimpse of Morris, Russell was decidedly intrigued. Morris was short and delicate; a boy-man with porcelain skin, wire-rimmed glasses, and baby-fine blond hair. Russell found something appealing in Morris's Lolita-in-distress air as he unsuccessfully tried to reach a book on the top shelf of a bookcase. Repeatedly, Morris attempted to jump up and grab the book. With each failed attempt, he appeared more dejected, desperate, and pouty.

Although Russell wasn't much taller than Morris, he stepped in to help, stretching to grab the book. It was *The Federal Reporter, Second Series*—a decidedly unromantic collection of U.S. appellate court case law.

"Thanks," said the soft-spoken Morris as Russell handed him the book. "Guess I needed a few extra inches."

"You're welcome," said Russell. "Glad to help. My name is Steve Russell."

"Pleasure to meet you, Steve Russell. My name is Phillip Morris."

"Great name. Are you related?"

"No, but people ask me that all the time."

"You don't look like you belong here, Phillip."

"Neither do you—and I don't belong here," Morris replied. He paused for a moment, then continued, "I noticed you earlier in the recreation room."

"Really?"

"Yes. I was hoping you'd speak to me."

"What do they have you in here for, Phillip?"

"I rented a car and kept it too long."

"Really? Did they charge you with auto theft?"

"No, it's called theft of service. Why are you here?"

"Insurance fraud."

"Damn, we're both in a mess, aren't we?"

"Could be worse."

"How's that? It's pretty bad already. At least for me it is."

"Well, Phillip, for one thing, I would have been worse off if I hadn't met you today."

"Well, you have to admit this is a hell of a place to meet for the first time," said Morris, ducking his head flirtatiously. "Plus, I'm kinda shy."

"I like shy," replied Russell.

"You're funny," said Morris with a smile.

"No, seriously, I like shy people," insisted Russell.

"I like you, too," said Morris.

"We sound like two schoolkids," said Russell, faking embarrassment.

"This could be good," said Morris.

"It will be," said Russell. "We can control how good it will be."

"Where are you from?"

"Virginia Beach, but I caught this insurance fraud case when I was living in Houston. You?"

"Arkansas, but I've been living in Houston and Galveston. Actually, I was fishing in Galveston when they arrested me."

"I like to fish, too. How in the world did you get arrested while fishing?"

"Long story. I'll tell you later."

Russell looked down at the book he had handed to Morris, *The Federal Reporter*. He then lied to Morris for the first time.

"I'm an attorney," Russell said. "What is it exactly that you're looking for? Maybe I can help."

Morris explained that he was doing a favor for a friend in his cellblock who wanted to file a federal appeal of his conviction. Like the half-dozen or so other inmates in the library, and quite possibly the rest of the jail's inhabitants, he was hunting for legal loopholes.

"Well, he can file it, but it's not going to work," said Russell in a knowledgeable tone. "First, he has to exhaust his state court remedies via Article 11.07 of the State Writ of Habeas Corpus Code."

Morris grabbed his yellow legal pad and furiously scribbled down this bit of information.

"What tank are you in?" Russell asked.

"9 A 5. How about you?"

"9 A 4," replied Russell, smiling.

"Right next door to each other!"

"Yeah, but they might as well be a thousand miles away."

"I sure wish you were in 9 A 5 with me," said Morris, already drawn to Russell and the confidence he exuded.

"Me, too. I might just be able to make that happen."

"Really?" asked Morris. "If you can pull that off, you really are pretty good."

"If you only knew some of the shit I've pulled off," bragged Russell. He was laying it on thick, but it didn't seem to matter to Morris.

"I never thought I would come to jail and meet someone I like."

"I never did either. You don't belong here, Phillip. I promise, I'll help you any way I can."

Since their allotted time in the library was about to expire, the two men exchanged names and jail identification numbers on slips of paper and agreed to meet later in the recreation room.

"Can it be a date?" Morris asked.

"Yeah, it can be a date," Russell said with a laugh.

"Wow! Our first date at prison rec. This is so romantic!"

"I'll see you in the rec room, Phillip Morris."

With that, the two prisoners, dressed in identical Day-Glo orange jumpsuits, disappeared back to their separate cellblocks. But Russell, who prides himself on reading people quickly, was already envisioning a future as Morris's protector and provider. Likewise, Morris had been impressed with Russell's knowledge of the law and flattered by his obvious interest in him. Russell seemed like a man who knew what he was doing, an appealing trait to an at-times helpless type like Morris. Morris was already beginning to feel beholden to, and somewhat mesmerized by, his new friend.

"The attraction I had at the beginning for Steve is a bit hard to explain," Morris tells me later. "As for a physical attraction, I can't say if there was one or not. I know that I had this incredible need or desire to be with him or near him at all times. He was a take-charge kind of guy. I guess you can say the attraction evolved and became stronger."

Unfortunately for the two prisoners, the Harris County Jail's rec-room scheduling did not concern itself with the romantic aspirations of Russell and Morris, and their date was postponed. Russell was determined not to lose contact, though, and he began writing to Morris daily. In the letters, Russell claimed he was a lawyer from Florida. He said he'd just been released from federal prison, which was true, after refusing to testify against the Mafia, which was not. He also told Morris that he reminded him of his former lover, who had recently died of AIDS.

Morris apparently believed it all. Like Russell, he was awaiting transfer from Harris County to a state prison. As he had told Russell, when he failed to return a rental car to a Houston agency in 1989, the agency had filed a theft-of-service charge against him. He was ordered to repay the rental agency and given a probated sentence of six years' deferred adjudication. It was his first brush with the law, and according to the terms of the sentence, had he stayed out of trouble for six years, he would have served no prison time and retained no criminal record. The sentence also called for Morris to hold a steady job. When he failed to do so, he was remanded to a restitution center, or halfway house, where his progress could be closely observed. There, according to Morris, he had a falling out with another resident—a large black man with an amputated foot—over God's view of homosexuality and Morris's declaration that he was an agnostic.

"He said I was a sinner," Morris recalls. "He told me he was going to 'blanket' me. That means throwing a blanket over my head, and then beating me with a board."

Alarmed by this prospect, the fragile Morris made alternate plans for the evening.

"I called a friend and asked him to wait in his car down the street from the center. Then I packed my suitcase, put it inside a large garbage bag, put it on a dolly, and then wheeled it past the staff, right out the front door, past the dumpster, and down the street."

The next morning, after the 35-year-old Morris called his probation officer to fill him in, a warrant was issued for his arrest.

After their first meeting in the jail law library, Russell sent jailhouse notes—or "kites," as they are called—to

Morris through other inmates. Within a few days, Russell arranged to have himself transferred to Morris's cell-block, an all-homosexual unit, by claiming that homophobes in his own jail pod were harassing him.

"Steven's letters had stopped coming," says Morris. "Then one day I turned around, and there he was. We saw each other and began to hug. That was the first time we had ever touched."

When viewed in light of their earlier experiences and relationships, the instant attraction between the two men is perfectly understandable—indeed, it seems almost inevitable.

chapter two

Anything He Wants

The son of a Baptist preacher, Phillip Morris was born on the evening of March 13, 1959—a Friday the 13th, as it happened.

"Now tell me that there's not some connection between me and Steven and the number thirteen," says Morris earnestly. "Steve has a lot of books that talk about reincarnation and past lives. About carrying yourself over from one life to another. He talks about there being no coincidences, and that everything happens for a reason."

With two older brothers and a younger sister, Morris grew up in Blythe, Arkansas, three miles from Memphis near the Mississippi River. His father and his uncle owned a business that distributed candy and cigars throughout Arkansas, Tennessee, and Missouri. Despite his parents' divorce and custody battles early in his life, he insists that his early years were pure bliss.

"I had a wonderful childhood. I couldn't have asked for a better childhood. My mother raised us, but she was kind of wild. Later, my dad got saved, and then he got ordained."

Although he left home during his senior year, Morris managed to finish high school, and even enrolled at Memphis State. After dropping out, he spent time in Atlanta, and then Dallas.

"In Dallas I hooked up with the executive producer of a Broadway musical as his executive assistant-slash-boyfriend. But basically he was just an old chicken hawk. We rode around in limousines, and I stayed drunk all the time. I was just nineteen years old. My job was a joke. It was just for show. That lasted about a year or so. But finally I got fed up with his bullshit, and he probably got fed up with mine."

Morris remained in Dallas, where, true to an emerging pattern, he soon teamed up with another generous provider, relying on his looks, charm, and vulnerability to cement his status as a kept man.

"He bought me cars, and took me on trips," he says of this next companion, whom he identifies only as "Mel." "He sent me to Hawaii for Christmas. He just spoiled me.

Anything I wanted, he bought. He was as obsessed with me as Steve is. He dressed me. He chose everything. It was like the Julia Roberts movie, *Sleeping With the Enemy*."

Mel was a full-blooded Apache, Morris says, about 6-foot-1, and obsessed with cleanliness. He had matching outfits handmade for the two of them.

"When you walked into my closet, everything was arranged according to the color spectrum, from the lightest color to the darkest. He had a thing about me in baseball shirts. He really liked me in sportswear. I had every NFL football jacket. And before I would go out, he'd ask me what I was going to wear. He was obsessed like that."

Like Steven Russell, Mel was also a con man, although Morris says that at the time he had no idea what Mel was up to.

"He was embezzling from this company and putting the money into an art gallery and a photography studio," Morris recalls. "But one of his partners turned him in. He found a check with the company's name on it, and he called the company and told them they had an employee stealing from them."

After Mel's arrest, Morris's life took an even stranger turn. This time, Morris says, one of Mel's friends kidnapped him.

"This was back before AIDS, in 1981," he says. "Mel and I were involved in ménages à trois back then, with both men and women. Well, this particular guy was one of the few people Mel liked. So Mel allowed me to go out with him and do whatever I wanted to.

"Anyway, this guy kidnapped me and kept me between a month and three months. I had no concept of time. He had a bodyguard. Anytime we left his house, I was always in the middle. I was never left alone. And I never had any money on me.

"Well, one day, he walked into this bank on Mockingbird Lane near the Stemmons Freeway. And when he walked through the second of two sets of glass doors, I managed to get back in the truck, which had a full tank of gas, and I drove straight to Longview, Texas."

From Longview, Morris quickly moved on to Atlanta, and after a few weeks Mel tracked him down there. He'd been released from jail, he claimed, and had cleaned up his act. He asked Phillip to come back to him, and Phillip did. Together, they relocated to Little Rock, but Mel remained tight-lipped about his business affairs. When Mel said to get in the car, Morris didn't ask why, or where they were going. One day, they drove from Little Rock to Memphis to Nashville. During their trips, Mel usually left Morris to wait in a hotel room. But this time, in Nashville, he pulled into the parking lot of a bank and went inside, leaving Morris alone in the car. A few minutes later, Morris saw Mel being marched out of the bank by a police officer. Other squad cars quickly converged on the bank. As Morris looked on, they took Mel away.

Luckily for Morris, Mel had left the keys in the car, so Morris got behind the wheel and drove all the way back to his friend's house in Longview. Not long after he arrived, Mel called. He had been extradited to Texas, made bail, and once again tracked Morris down. He told Morris he would stop by soon to pick him up.

By now, though, Morris had had enough. When Mel arrived, the police were waiting for him, and arrested him for violating the terms of his bond.

After that, Morris drifted to Houston, a city with a surprisingly large gay population centered around the near-downtown neighborhood of Montrose. Houston is a Mecca to many young gay men and women from Texas and elsewhere, a place where they can live their lives without apology, and Phillip Morris had many friends there. Unfortunately, his stop in Houston would also bring on his mishap with the rental car company, which, in turn, led to his problems at the halfway house and his incarceration at Harris County Jail.

After Morris's deferred adjudication was revoked, he was ordered to serve four years in state prison. At the time, because of prison overcrowding in Texas, it was unlikely he would actually do more than nine months of hard time. Similarly, Russell's three-year sentence would probably be served in about six months. In Russell's mind, it would be tolerable if there was a chance that he and Morris might have a future together on the outside. So Russell set about making that a reality.

"Steven was a take-charge kind of guy," says Morris. "He was strong, and he knew the ropes, and could get anything done. I cried all day every day [in jail], and whined all the time. He made me feel safe and assured me that everything was going to be okay."

Russell patiently tolerated Morris's crying jags, and offered him a choice of three attorneys to represent him, promising to cover his legal fees. In the less-than-private confines of the county lock-up, the two men soon consummated their attraction.

"We fell in love with each other at the county jail," Russell says. "The first three months we were together were like a honeymoon."

At the beginning of the fourth month, Russell jokes, the cell's close quarters began to take their toll. "We had to use the toilet in front of each other day after day," he says, "and I remember at one point Phillip turning to me and saying, 'Honey, I think the honeymoon is over.'"

While their passion may have subsided, or at least been put on hold, the sense of partnership and trust between the two blossomed. In phone conversations from jail, Morris told one of his friends on the outside about his new boyfriend; that he was a lawyer, that he was looking after him, that the two of them were going to make a life together once they were released.

"I told him that Steve had said the three special words to me," Morris recalls: "'Anything you want.'"

The more Morris relied on Russell, the more protective Russell became of him. At one point, Morris complained to Russell about a fellow inmate who screamed incessantly. The round-the-clock screeching kept Morris from sleeping, and he couldn't stand it anymore. Not long afterward, Morris, a diabetic, was returning from the infirmary after receiving his regular insulin shot when he found a crowd of inmates gathered around his cell watching a fight. One of the participants was the screamer, and he wasn't faring well.

"When I asked what was going on," Morris says, "someone told me that Steve had paid someone to beat him up."

In the wake of this incident, Harris County officials moved Russell to another cellblock to await his transfer to state custody. When it came time for Russell to "catch the chain" and board the bus that would take him to the state prison system, he was pleased to discover that Morris was making the trip, too.

The no frills state-owned-and-operated bus—customized to resemble a long, large mobile prison cell—carrying Russell and Morris was headed for Huntsville. Seventy-five miles north of Houston, Huntsville is headquarters for the Texas Department of Criminal Justice, as well as the home of seven of its prison units, including the Diagnostic Unit. There, inmates are processed, evaluated and sorted by degree of dangerousness and length of sentence. After a few weeks, each gets assigned to one of the 60 or so prison facilities scattered around Texas that house the state's approximately 150,000 convicted felons.

After a month together at Diagnostic, and a total of nearly six months of jailhouse romance, Russell and Morris were separated. In June 1995, Morris was assigned to the Ramsey 2 Unit, and Russell to the Ramsey 3, both just south of Houston.

Russell again promised Morris that he would take care of him when they were both free men on parole, and he became obsessed with fulfilling that promise. Indeed, he was obsessed with everything about Morris. More than anything else, Russell appreciated Morris's loyalty—the most prized value in Russell's personal code of ethics.

"Studying people is a large part of what I do," Russell says. "I study their habits and routines. When I talk to someone, I watch their eyes to see if they're looking me in the eye or if they're drifting off somewhere else. I have to know that I can trust them before I know I can get them to trust me. Phillip is my lover, best friend, soul mate, life partner, and the only person in this entire world who totally understands me. I trust him with everything, and our love is unconditional. He is extremely intuitive, and protects me from myself. I protect him from anyone who even thinks about harming him in any way. And I have a very long memory. God help anyone who makes the mistake of trying to drive a wedge between us, or tries to inject their thoughts or opinions into our relationship. Phillip forgives and forgets. I forgive, but I never forget."

Russell knew that both he and Morris would be paroled from prison by the end of 1995 at the latest. The risk was too great, and the rewards too small, to bother with an escape. During his three-month stay at Ramsey 3 Unit in Rosharon, Texas, Russell was a model prisoner.

After serving nine months of his three-year sentence, Russell was paroled. In October 1995, he immediately began making plans to set up house with Morris, who still had two months to serve before he became eligible for parole. They had continued to write to each other daily, and eagerly anticipated the time when they would reunite without the company of guards and steel bars. Russell was determined that, when that day arrived, he and Morris would live high and wide.

In the meantime, to keep his parole officer satisfied,

Russell took on three low-level jobs in Houston. He worked in the deli departments at two different supermarkets, Randall's and Kroger's, and he clerked the front desk at the Red Roof Inn near Hobby Airport. Later he was hired on part-time (at $23 an hour) with an outfit that provided local companies with temporary clerical help. But Russell had more ambitious plans as well—and an illicit nest egg to help get him started.

After settling into an apartment on Space Center Boulevard in Houston's Clear Lake area, Russell claims he contacted a friend of his and his late boyfriend, James Kemple. After Jimmy's AIDS-related death in July 1994, Russell and the friend had stayed in touch.

On the phone, Russell told the friend that although federal and Florida investigators thought they had discovered all of the life insurance policies that he had illegally taken out while impersonating Jimmy, there was still one more remaining. Written by Banker's Life Assurance in Miami, it named the friend as beneficiary.

"It was for $50,000," says Russell. "[The friend] agreed to cash the policy in, and we split the money."

Russell well knew, however, that $25,000 would not last long given the lifestyle he envisioned for himself and Morris. Russell had grown up privileged with plenty of material comforts. For the most part, he had lived in upscale homes, driven high-end cars, and led an extremely com-

fortable life. It was a lifestyle he wanted Morris to experience, and it would require more than $25,000. Alas, Rus-
sell couldn't just quit his make-do jobs and explain to his
parole officer that he didn't need to work because he'd collected on a fraudulently obtained insurance policy. Before
he could quit those jobs, he'd need a better one. As usual,
Russell had a plan.

In the Harris County jail, Russell had told Morris that
he was an attorney; he now expanded this fabrication.
He began his ruse by visiting Morris, still housed at
Ramsey 2, while posing as the fictional Steve Rousseau,
attorney-at-law.

"By doing that, my visitation time was unlimited," he
says. Relatives and friends can only visit prisoners once a
week, for no longer than two hours. "And I could schedule them around my three jobs instead of having to come
during regular visiting hours."

The deceit didn't stop at that. Still identifying himself as
Rousseau, he telephoned the parole office and arranged to
have Morris's release date moved up a month.

"I sent the lady [in the parole office] a dozen roses," he
says.

Morris was now set to be released on the afternoon of
December 1, but Russell still wasn't satisfied. Based on his
own experience with the parole process, Russell knew
Morris would not be released until sometime between

3:00 and 4:00 P.M. from the Huntsville Unit, through which all inmates are processed before release. On November 30, 1995, "Rousseau" phoned the warden at Huntsville. Morris needed to appear in federal court the next morning, Russell lied, and he would appreciate it if he could pick up his client at 8:30 A.M., rather than in the afternoon. The warden, known as an amiable man, told Russell he'd have Morris ready for him the next morning.

True to his word, the warden handed Morris over to Russell early the next morning. After thanking the warden, Russell and Morris drove west on state Highway 30 out of downtown Huntsville, and over to Interstate 45 toward Houston. Before heading south on the interstate, they stopped at a Denny's for a big celebratory breakfast.

After breakfast, Russell and Morris drove to a Galveston motel. Russell bought two dozen spicy cold boiled shrimp and a bottle of Moët champagne. This soon became typical. While they lived together in the Clear Lake apartment, the pair frequently indulged in hotel getaways.

"Our favorite routine was to check into a motel on Friday night," says Russell. "Phillip didn't give a shit where, just so long as it was a nice, clean motel."

"We made several weekend trips," says Morris. "Sometimes just checking into a hotel there in Houston. But it was always like a honeymoon."

Ten days after Morris's release, Russell decided on a grander splurge. He and Morris flew to Miami, and then drove to Key West, where they rented a house with a pool and a 24-foot motorboat. They swam, snorkeled, and sunbathed. They took the boat island-hopping through the Keys. They shopped on touristy Duval Street in Key West. Evenings, they went to restaurants and bars, or rented movies and stayed home. They also almost lost their lives.

"One of the most exciting times I've ever had was when we were halfway to Cuba and got caught in this terrible storm," says Morris. "There were boats capsizing, and helicopters flying everywhere. Waves about 20 feet high were coming over our little boat."

Having grown up on the waters of Virginia and North Carolina, Russell could pilot boats skillfully.

"My suggestion was to try and outrun the storm," Morris says. "His was to head straight into it. We probably would have been shark bait if he'd listened to me."

Near-drowning aside, Morris says he felt safe all the while on the trip. It was almost like a honeymoon. Russell too seemed content, at least initially, as his entries in a sporadic log he kept of the journey reveal.

"Left today for Key West," he wrote on December 11. "PM and I have dreamed about this trip for so long and now it has finally come to reality. I love him so much. I become quite aggravated with myself when I make some pretty stupid comments. PM always seems to understand me better than I do myself at times. I am so happy I have someone who loves me so much."

December 12: "I find myself so turned on by PM. I love massaging his body.... I feel really bad for him that he hasn't been able to perform as I have. I do believe that after his time [in prison] his body needs healing. Diabetes makes sexual activity a real struggle. He does completely satisfy me like no one else has been able to despite our somewhat short time of 12 days with complete freedom. I really enjoy his smile. It helps me through the day."

Eight days later, judging by Russell's notes, things were less idyllic.

December 20: "Worst day yet. The early part went well as we had a great dinner and watched *Forrest Gump*. After the movie, PM asked me to go out for a drink, which I readily wanted to do, but now regret. I can't drink. I know better. I am awful upset with myself for even trying. I believe the same holds true for PM. He is a totally different person [when he drinks], and I do not like this side of him. I've spent more time in gay bars in the past 20 days than I have in the past five years, and I'm getting tired of it. All this drinking does is put a strain on our relationship and ruin the following day because we are both too ill to get out of bed. I feel this explosion coming, and if this continues to happen, I know I will react by leaving him. At 3 A.M. he decided to go eat and stayed out the rest of the night after an argument and kicking the shit out of me. We both apologized the next morning."

December 21: "Went out on the boat and explored several islands. Nice day compared to the others except it was cold. I enjoyed the relaxation with PM. He is so beautiful. He loves me so much. I am so determined to be a great lover to him so he will never know what abandonment or sadness is ever again."

December 22: "Dreamed about my dad last night. As usual it was confrontational—always lecturing and telling me what to do."

December 24: "Let's forget this day ever happened."

December 25: "Dreamed last night that PM was in a wreck. The police arrested him and told him he was a parole violator. I grabbed him from the police and woke up holding onto him for dear life while also scaring him to death."

Also on Christmas Day, Russell wrote of his irritation at some of Morris's habits: "Today was a lazy day. PM recovered with a hangover from Christmas Eve. We watched a record 5 movies all of which were enjoyed. PM really beats himself up when he drinks and I only make matters worse when I put in my 2 cents worth. I am quite concerned about his blood sugar and the side effects of alcohol, food and smoking. I know he doesn't want to do any of the

three but there seems to be a compelling reason he continues. I have to learn that he is not like my previous relationships. He is extremely intelligent. I only hope he will use
that intelligence to take care of himself.... One thing I do
truly believe is [Morris's] loyalty to me. I don't think I ever
had a more loyal friend or lover. While he enjoys looking
and smiling at others, his heart and mind are with me,
which truly relieves my mind.... He told me yesterday that
he is thinking about going back on Prozac. We both con-
tinue to battle depression."

December 26: "Started Prozac."

The vacation over, Russell and Morris flew back to Houston and the apartment Russell had leased for them in
Clear Lake. It was an upstairs unit on the second floor of
a complex near the Johnson Space Center.

Although Morris perpetuated the joke among their
friends that Russell's only goal in life was to make him
happy, Morris insists that he really asked for very little.
On his birthday on March 13, 1996, Morris told Russell
that all he wanted was a puppy.

"He put me in the truck," Morris says, "and we drove
to a house where there were some five- to six-week-old
Min Pins [miniature Doberman Pinschers] for sale. We
went into the backyard, and I'm on the ground playing
with all of these puppies. And I had picked out the one I

wanted, when I looked over and saw the tiniest, cutest red Min Pin from a different litter. I told the owner that I wanted her, too. She fit in the palm of my hand!"

Russell bought both dogs. They named them Alex and Lucy.

At first Russell and Morris ate out most nights. But soon Russell began cooking more at home, partly because of his concern about Morris's diabetes, and partly because he didn't like the frequent trips back into the inner city to eat at the trendy restaurants in the Montrose area. At home, in addition to the cooking, Russell did all the grocery shopping, a chore Morris hated. On almost every supermarket trip, Russell would find some new gadget to buy. Evenings were spent on the huge couch, sometimes watching television, more often just talking—at least when Russell wasn't hard at work on his next big scheme or project to get rich quick.

"Living with Steve was like living with a big ball of energy," says Morris. "He always had to be doing something."

Clear Lake was a good 30 miles or so out the Gulf Freeway from downtown. Its main drag, NASA Road 1, is a terminally congested thoroughfare lined by fast food drive-ins. Despite access to Russell's internal fountain of adrenaline, Morris sometimes missed his adopted home turf in Montrose. Ostensibly a residential neighborhood,

Montrose is a vibrant mixture of young professionals, street people (some dangerous, some in danger), adult bookstores, boutiques, upscale restaurants, fast food joints, antique shops, churches, tattoo parlors, restored homes, gaudy new condos, and gay, straight, and bisexual bars. It's a testament to Houston's minimal zoning laws.

More so than Russell, Morris was a social animal. He was eager to contact old friends, and introduce them to his new lover. Among the people Russell came to know best were Morris's sister, Pam Beckham, and two of Morris's former neighbors, Gaynelle Hollenhead and Duane Nowell. Nowell, like Morris, was a gay man who drifted in and out of employment. Hollenhead was an elderly woman who owned her own home and had often played hostess to Morris and Nowell. When Morris introduced Russell to Hollenhead as an attorney, she seemed skeptical.

"How can you still be an attorney if you've just gotten out of prison?" she asked.

His crime, Russell explained, had not been severe enough to cost him his law license. This was, of course, grade-A bullshit—but it was enough to appease Hollenhead. She even confided to Russell that she was having legal problems of her own, butting heads with an architect over how much money she owed him for work done on her house. The case was headed for mediation.

Emboldened by his recent success posing as Morris's attorney, Russell offered to represent Hollenhead. She accepted, and on her scheduled court day, Hollenhead met Russell at the Harris County Civil Courthouse. Russell, wearing a three-piece suit, arrived late, explaining that he had been tied up on a case at a different court. Then, just like all the real attorneys, he walked back into the judge's chambers. A few minutes later, he returned to the courtroom. Hollenhead, Russell, the architect, the architect's attorney, and a mediator then gathered in a small conference room. Two hours later, they emerged with a payment schedule agreeable to both Hollenhead and the architect.

On their way out of the courthouse, Russell could hardly contain his pleasure with his performance. "Didn't I do great?" he asked Hollenhead excitedly. "Didn't I do great?"

It seemed a strange question for an attorney to ask. "You did fine," Hollenhead replied.

More confident than ever of his ability to convince anyone of anything, Russell felt prepared to enter a world where he knew his skill as a con artist would be appropriately rewarded. He was ready to join the ranks of Fortune 500 management. In some ways, he felt he was just following his natural calling. After all, his whole life began with a lie.

chapter three

The Early Years

Steven Jay Russell's birth certificate says he was born on Saturday, September 14, 1957, at Albemarle Hospital in Elizabeth City, North Carolina, which is true. It is also true, as stated on the birth certificate, that Russell was delivered at 12:01 A.M. (He likes to point out that had he emerged just 61 seconds earlier, he would have been born on Friday the 13th, just like Phillip Morris.) But contrary to what is stated on the birth certificate David and Georgia Russell kept in their possession, they were not Steven's biological parents.

According to birth records at the Pasquotank County courthouse in Elizabeth City, Steven was actually born

Steven Jay Basham. Shortly after his birth the Russells adopted him. David Russell was a small, dark-haired, inherently conservative man who, with his brother Warren, ran one of the area's largest produce companies. His equally compact and raven-haired wife was an independent, serious-minded woman who had trained as a registered nurse at DePaul Hospital in Norfolk. Almost ten years before Steven was born, Georgia Russell had given birth to a son. The delivery had left her unable to have more children. She desperately wanted another child.

Steven was only five days old when the Russells, both now deceased, went to Albemarle Hospital to claim the infant as their second son. In a suspicious exchange in the hospital parking lot, Steven's birth mother actually handed him over to Georgia. Georgia Russell's sister, Leona Williams, was present during the transaction. She says that, in those days, North Carolina law required a woman giving up a baby for adoption had to literally physically hand the child to the adoptive mother. However, a check of the history of North Carolina adoption laws reveals no such bizarre requirement. Georgia and David Russell are now dead, and Steven's birth mother declined to talk to me for this book. So exactly what was going on in that parking lot—and how legal those arrangements were—remains unclear.

Leona Williams, 80 years old at the time I interviewed

her, recalls no extraordinary reaction or emotion on the part of either the birth mother or Steven during the baby exchange, but she says her sister and brother-in-law were overjoyed.

"She and Dave were so happy," says Williams. "They had waited so long for this. It was a glorious occasion. He was so precious. There just aren't words to describe how precious."

After taking custody of the baby at Albemarle Hospital, the Russells headed back across the state line to their home in Virginia Beach, Virginia, a 45-mile drive from Elizabeth City along the George Washington Highway. Elizabeth City is a small, quiet community in the low-slung lands of the northeast portion of the state—part of the Tidewater area that extends northward into Virginia. It is located near the beautiful but treacherous Great Dismal Swamp, an aptly named 200,000-acre wilderness area. The George Washington Highway is a scenic stretch of road that follows the path of the Great Dismal Swamp Canal, which, like the history of the Russell clan, spans both states. The waterway, for which Washington turned the first spade of dirt when construction began in 1793, is a 22-mile canal that connects the Chesapeake Bay in Virginia with the Pasquotank River and Albemarle Sound in North Carolina. It is the oldest operating artificial waterway in the United States.

According to the managers of the wildlife refuge, although the average depth of the swamp's amber-colored water is only six feet, it is unusually pure—preserved by tannic acids from the bark of juniper, gum and cypress trees. Before the advent of refrigeration, water from the swamp was a valued commodity aboard sailing ships, as it could be stored in kegs and remained fresh on long voyages. Some residents of the region even told stories of the magical qualities of the swamp water—that if consumed regularly, it would promote health and longevity.

Of course, the extra-medicinal qualities of the water from the Great Dismal Swamp are, at best, debatable; stories about the healing powers of the water may very well have been part of some early Tidewater area con job. Or perhaps there is something in the brackish water that encourages tall tales—something that seeped into the blood, and into the psyche, of young Steven Russell as he made his way back and forth along that early Tidewater commerce route on the eastern edge of the swamp during the first two decades of his life. It is, after all, a route with a long history in the Russell clan.

According to the family's lore, Steven Russell's grandfather, D.S. Russell, left his home in Scotland in the late 1800s at the age of 14 as a stowaway aboard a schooner. When the vessel shipwrecked off the coast of North Carolina's Cape Hatteras, the teenager miraculously swam ashore, and was taken in and raised by the generous people of Avon, North Carolina. After marrying a local girl, the Scotsman moved up the coast to Norfolk, where he began selling produce out of a cart on the streets of the city. By the time his sons Warren and David—Steven's adoptive father—joined him in the business, it had blossomed into one of the largest wholesale produce outfits in the Tidewater area. Steve Russell, as well as his older adoptive brother Scott, would also eventually work at D.S. Russell & Sons, which, during each of its last two years of operation, had revenues of $6 million. Not bad for a family business that began on the sidewalks of Norfolk.

"From the time he was real young he was down there," says Steven's uncle, Herscal Williams (Leona's husband). "And Steven appeared to like it, and was good at it. They had a good business." But it was not Steven Russell's early childhood dream to follow his forebears into the produce business. Instead, say his Aunt Leona and Russell himself, as a small boy, he wanted to drive a garbage truck.

From that first day at the hospital, Herscal and Leona Williams, who are now retired and live in Elizabeth City, felt especially close to Steven. Leona still remembers her young nephew climbing up the back porch steps of their old house. She and Herscal lived only a few blocks up the street from the Russells in the resort town of Virginia

Beach, adjacent to Norfolk and the crab-filled waters of the Chesapeake Bay.

"He was just a tiny fellow, but he'd get up on our back porch, and he would get so excited when the garbage men would come by," says Leona, a sweet, gray-haired woman with a quavering voice. "And he'd say, 'When I get big, I want to be a garbage man.'"

Since they lived in the same neighborhood, and since Steven's parents often took vacations to the Carolinas and Florida, the Williamses frequently acted as willing babysitters for Steven. The boy loved the Williamses as if they were another set of parents, and they felt just as strongly about him. Leona remembers him as a smart and adventurous little boy who was interested in everything. She did not approve of Steven's long blond hair, though.

"He was such a handsome child," says Leona. "He had these beautiful blond curls. But back then boys didn't wear long hair. So I thought, 'He's got curls, but I'd rather he didn't.' So I took him to the barbershop. It was his first haircut, and he was overjoyed."

Steven's mother, however, was not. She began weeping as soon as she saw her three-year-old son.

For the most part, according to Russell, David and Georgia could not have been better parents. The Russells were devoted to their two sons, and to each other.

"My dad was in love with my mom and vice versa,"

Steven says. "I've never seen or been around a hetero couple who cared for each other more."

Russell remembers his father being the dominant parent in his early childhood, a strict disciplinarian with an occasional flash of temper. But during Russell's teenage years, he says, his mother starting calling most of the shots. Dave Russell became more passive and it was left to Georgia to mete out discipline. She also decided where the family would live, where they would go, and whom they would see. Both parents loved to travel, and Georgia disliked cooking, so they preferred to eat in restaurants instead of at home.

As a child, Steven spent free time with his dad, mostly at the produce company. After leaving from her nursing job in the afternoon, Georgia would pick up Steven at public school and drive him to "the store"—their produce warehouse in Norfolk. There he played, helped prepare orders for delivery, and fielded phone orders. Soon, though, he outgrew his interest in manual labor, preferring a grander stage as an imaginary high rolling wheeler-dealer.

"My immature ass thought I was supposed to be running the produce company at fourteen years old," he says. "I wanted to be sitting behind a desk instead of putting up the orders."

Early on, Russell demonstrated aptitude in both math

and music, and he quickly grasped the fundamentals of accounting and money management (tools that would come in handy in some of his later "ventures"). Starting at age five, Steven studied at the Marsh School of Music in Norfolk, where, during eight years of lessons, he became quite accomplished at the piano and organ. The lessons began over the objections of his father, who feared that a boy who gravitated to the arts instead of sports would be labeled a sissy. David Russell had first expressed concern about this when Steven was a toddler, and his wife had dressed up the boy with the long blond locks as a little girl. But Georgia won out this time, and it wasn't long before Steven won first place in a children's piano competition in Norfolk.

Outside of his family, Russell had little companionship. He claims he was "too busy to be bothered with other children." He hated their games and most of their toys, with the exception of big rig trucks. His brother, Scott, whom Steven describes as a quiet, intelligent boy who excelled at playing eight-ball pool, went out of his way to include Steven in his adventures, although he was nearly ten years his senior. (Scott Russell now lives in San Antonio, Texas, where he works in the wholesale tomato industry. While Steven speaks admiringly of his older brother, Scott declined several requests to talk with me about Steven.) In addition to pool halls, Scott occasionally took Steven along with him on his dates, and to a local garage where he always seemed to be working on his latest sports car.

Steven and his father occasionally went fishing at one of the many beaches in the area. David Russell taught his son how to surf cast. At their house in Virginia Beach, the family kept a small motorboat in the backyard and often took it out fishing for gray trout in the Chesapeake Bay, only minutes away by car. When it came to competitive sports, though, Russell was hopeless. His mother tried to get him interested in basketball, going so far as to install a hoop in the backyard. Her efforts didn't take.

"I couldn't hit a basket if parole was attached," Russell says with a laugh.

Russell does claim to be an excellent shot with firearms. Prior to his first adult felony arrest, which barred him from legally possessing them, he owned several handguns, rifles, and shotguns. His mother and father approved of this interest.

But it was his interest in fires—particularly in setting them—that really got their attention. The fires began shortly after Steven received some news that shocked him. He was only nine at the time, but he still remembers his mother calling him into the den.

"Steve, your dad and I need to talk to you about something very important," Georgia began gently. "There are some children that are born of their parents, and other children that are chosen by their parents."

"Okay," Steven said.

"You are a very special child, because you were chosen by me and your dad," she continued. "Remember me telling you that you were born in Elizabeth City?"

"Yes."

"Well, that's where we got you from another person, from the woman who actually gave birth to you. Your biological mom. Her name is Brenda. She gave you to us just days after you were born, and you've been with us ever since. Have you ever heard of adoption, Steve?"

Silence.

"Honey, your dad and I adopted you from Brenda, and we love you so very much," said Georgia in her most maternal and nurturing voice. "We think it's important for us to tell you that you were adopted so you hear it from us, and so you understand that we love you as much as we love Scott. Do you understand what I'm telling you?"

"Okay," Steven replied numbly.

"Being adopted is a gift to us, and a gift to you," said Georgia, trying hard to get through to Steven. "So many babies are born and not loved by their parents. Your dad and I love you very much."

"Where is Brenda now?" Steven asked.

"We don't know," said Georgia. "There shouldn't be any more contact between her and us and you. When you get older, we'll try to explain this to you some more, and help answer any other questions you have."

"I don't care," said Steven. "You and daddy are my parents."

"We also bought you a book about adoption and chosen children," said Georgia, handing him a volume he would never open and whose name he can't recall.

"Thank you," he said.

"Does this upset you, Steve?"

"No," he lied. "Does Scott know I'm adopted?"

"Yes."

"It's okay. I was just wondering."

"Honey, if this upsets you, or if you need to talk to me or your dad, we're here for you. We just both thought it would be best to tell you so that you would know. So that you wouldn't hear it from someone else first. We love you very much."

The conversation left Steven stunned. He felt overwhelmed with insecurity, and betrayed by his biological family. Soon afterward, he began having trouble concentrating in school. Some of his cousins teased him mercilessly. Steven decided to get even by torching their father's garage. They never teased him again.

Not long after that, he set another fire, this time burning another student's leather jacket at school. In 12-year-old Steven's eyes, the coat's owner bragged about the jacket, and about his athletic prowess, too much. "I can still remember the humiliation of always being the last person chosen to play soccer, football or softball," he says. To set the jacket ablaze, Russell first ignited a cotton jacket to help the leather one catch fire. The blaze also burned a classroom wall, causing more than $1,600 in damage. After this, some family members say, David and Georgia began to fear Steven.

The boy had gotten his revenge, but at a price. In the wake of the second incident, a Virginia juvenile court judge ordered Steven to report to the psychiatric ward of Norfolk General Hospital for 30 days of observation. During his month there, Steven was terrified. The only child in the mental ward, he watched in fear as the resident adults shuffled psychotically up and down the halls, and he listened with horror to their tales of electroshock therapy. His saving grace was a female nurse who made sure the adults kept their hands off him.

Reasoning that Steven needed special counseling, his parents turned to their minister, the Reverend Lamar Sentell of the Calvary Temple Church in Norfolk. Sentell is a larger-than-life, old-time-religion character who mixes a fire-and-brimstone message just this side of Pentecostalism with equal amounts of folksy Southern charm and the (conditional) promise of eternal salvation. For 25 years on radio and seven years on television, Sentell spread his version of the gospel over Tidewater airwaves. The gist of his message: that his brand of religion is the one and only true one, all others literally be damned.

The modest brick structure that is Calvary Temple Church is situated amid the abundant pines just off Norfolk's Military Highway (named for the community's leading employer). Although Sentell's church services are no longer broadcast, ON AIR signs still perch above the entrances to the church's sanctuary.

Steven initially grew up in a religiously mixed family, his father a Methodist, his mother with Assembly of God. After hearing Sentell's live broadcasts every morning on WCMS Radio, the Russells began attending Sentell's Fox Hall Southern Baptist Church in Norfolk. When Sentell broke with the Southern Baptist Conference, which he viewed as too liberal, the Russells followed him to Calvary Temple. Sentell recalls that the Russells had been attending his church for a couple of years when they asked him to help with Steven.

"I counseled with Steve for quite a spell," says Sentell, a tall man with a ruddy complexion who slicks his reddish gray hair straight back. "He finally grew out of [setting fires] to a degree, but they put him in a hospital. A psychiatric hospital. And those things are as dangerous as a rattlesnake."

Thirty-odd years later, Sentell still seems pained by the memory of seeing Steven in the hospital mental ward, and he has an especially vivid recollection of one of his visits. Just by coincidence, says Sentell, several fire department units were also dispatched to the medical facility that day.

"We were sitting in his room when, all of a sudden, fire trucks pulled up out front," Sentell says. "We were on the ninth floor, and I thought I was going to have to grab him and hold him to keep him from jumping out the window. I'm not kidding you. I mean he went crazy as a lunatic."

After his 30 days at Norfolk General, Steven was sent to school at Hanover Boys Home (now the Hanover Juvenile Correctional Center) for anger management therapy. He hated Hanover, and remembers it now as "the worst place in the world" and "a school for perverts." He was especially disturbed by the daily sight of some of the boys having sex in the showers. At 12 years old, Steven was skinny and small for his age, a perfect target for physical abuse at the hands of older, bigger boys.

Steven also hated the strict discipline and corporal punishment at Hanover. Whenever someone was caught breaking a rule, he says, the keepers would put him through a night of physical exercise, or beat him across the back with a strap. There were no locks on the dormitory doors, but it felt like prison just the same. He thought constantly about ways to escape.

During his nine months at Hanover, Steven came across two important pieces of information. First, after he took an IQ test, he and his parents learned that he had scored an exceptionally high 163. The school principal encouraged the Russells to transfer their son from Hanover to a place with a better academic climate. Content to let someone else deal with Steven's problems for while, the Russells declined. It was a decision that troubled the boy's Aunt Leona.

"I've always felt that maybe if he had gotten more counseling, if he had been shown more love, that maybe things would have turned out differently," she says. "But that was at a time when if you showed a difference in your personality, you were persecuted more than helped. Back then, anyone who was different, instead of getting help, you were just put aside."

Steven himself concurs.

"I was filled with rage for having to remain in that hellhole," he says.

It was also at Hanover that Steven had his first voluntary homosexual experience. His partner was a 17-year-old boy from Winchester, Virginia, who worked in the dining hall and encouraged the frail and malnourished-looking 12-year-old to eat.

"He was very sweet to me," Russell says fondly of the experience, which he refers to as "an awakening."

Their encounters began when a wrestling match on the school's football field led to the older boy performing oral sex on Steven. The next day, his friend paid him a visit in the school library. Sitting next to Steven, the older boy opened a copy of *National Geographic* on the table in front of them to photographs of naked black women, and started rubbing Steven's leg with his hand. A few minutes later, he was under the table for a replay of the previous day's activity.

"The next day he came back to library and saw me again," Russell says. "In fact, he visited me every single day until I left that fucking dump."

Russell enjoyed the encounters, but they also filled him with guilt, and he became even more determined to find some way to escape from Hanover.

While visiting his family during the Christmas break in 1970, Steven found an unlikely ticket to freedom when he got braces on his teeth. After returning to Hanover, he complained about them constantly, and his counselor had to drive him repeatedly to the nearest orthodontist, 30 miles away in Richmond. Just as Steven had hoped, the counselor soon advised the court and his parents that Steven was making great progress in dealing with his anger. He was sent home from Hanover on May 13, 1971, a

Friday. From then on, he would consider the 13th of the month, especially if it fell on a Friday, his lucky day.

Following his return from Hanover, Russell enrolled in high school at Tidewater Christian Academy, where Reverend Sentell was the superintendent. Russell began playing organ every Sunday at Sentell's church. Russell acknowledges that the minister played an influential role in his life, Sentell's hard line on morality notwithstanding.

"If you don't agree with Lamar's theology," Russell says, "he thinks you're going to hell. As a child, I knew nothing else. As an adult, I know he's totally wrong. However, I love the man dearly as a person. He was always so very kind to me."

His time at reform school, Russell says, contributed greatly to the sense of abandonment that had begun growing in him when he learned of his adoption. As he grew older, he became obsessed with the need to track down his biological family.

But his Aunt Leona insists she was aware of insecurity deep within her nephew much earlier. When Steven saw his mother weeping over his lost locks, for instance, he too began to cry. While some children cry out of immediate anger or discomfort, Leona got the impression that Steven's sobbing came from somewhere deep inside. Whenever his parents were due to return from a trip,

Steven would become so anxious in his anticipation that when they arrived, all he could do was hug them and cry.

"Steve could be hurt so easily," Leona says. "He was very sensitive. If anyone showed him resentment, like a teacher, he could be so deeply hurt. I can still almost hear that sob. It was never an outcry like a child throwing a tantrum. Just a sob from down here."

She presses her hand over her heart as she speaks.

chapter four

The Making
of a Con Man

After nine months at Hanover, Russell was happy to return to something resembling a normal life. Although he had an idea of his true sexual preference, he did his best to conceal it from his family and everyone else. Like many parents of their generation, David and Georgia Russell had been far from adept at handling such matters as sex education. Their entire efforts in that direction amounted to giving Steven a book entitled *Almost 13*.

At Tidewater Christian Academy, Steven didn't dare attempt liaisons with any of his new classmates. Instead, he occasionally ventured into bathroom stalls in shopping malls and parks or secluded spots in downtown

Norfolk for encounters with other boys or older men.

When Russell was 16, his grandfather was diagnosed with Alzheimer's disease. Often in the middle of the night, Steven's grandmother would call David and Georgia for help with her increasingly confused husband. More often than not, the Russells would dispatch Steven to his grandparents' house near the produce plant in Norfolk.

"After I took care of getting Daddy Dave calmed down, I would cruise downtown in my father's Cadillac," he says. "I'd cruise until I saw a guy that I liked, and would let him give me a blow job. I didn't participate other than that. Then."

By outward appearances, the former delinquent was now a model of Southern boyhood. By his mid-teen years, Steven was still slender and as tall as most boys in his class. His blond baby hair had turned brown, and his once round face took on longer, sharper features.

Steven often spent summers on Cape Hatteras in North Carolina, where his aunt and uncle, Ruby and Andrew Shanklin, owned a couple of motels. Often Ruby and "Shank" would accompany Russell's parents on their frequent Florida vacations. As he got older, his parents allowed Steven to spend that time under the watch of his cousin Gary, who was Shank and Ruby's boy, on the Cape.

For Steven, these were dream vacations. Gary, four years older, took him for rides on the beach in his Jeep, and introduced him to local girls. Russell went on his first date at age 15 in the back of Gary's car with a girl he met in a Hatteras pool room. The evening consisted mainly of listening to the radio as Gary displayed the speed and road-handling prowess of his new 1972 Ford Grand Torino. But, more importantly, it also marked Russell's first taste of heterosexual romance. His date was a 16-year-old girl, from Avon, North Carolina. Back at Tidewater Academy, Russell had dated several girls. He didn't go out with any for very long, nor did he have intercourse or make out with any of them, though he says each of them sexually excited him. This time, however, he would be more than excited.

"She was blond-haired, blue-eyed and sexy as hell," remembers Russell. "Gary took us all to see a movie at the Stratford Avon Theatre, but I was too busy kissing her to remember what the movie it was. That's also when I got my first handful of titty."

Gary worked some evenings as a deckhand on a 125-foot ferry boat that transported cars from Hatteras to Ocracoke Island, and sometimes late at night, after the captain had had a few drinks, Steven would take the helm and pilot the vessel across Hatteras Inlet and back.

One humid night, Steven and Gary drove up to nearby Rodanthe, on the northern end of the cape, for a late-night clandestine rendezvous with one of Gary's girlfriends at a local gas station. When the girl's father showed up instead, a chase ensued. A Chevy Blazer barreled into the parking lot while Steven was standing outside Gary's car, urinating. As soon as Steven saw the Blazer, he smelled trouble, and he pissed all over himself trying to zip up his jeans and jump back into Gary's car. "Get the fuck out of here," Steven screamed at Gary.

The two would-be Romeos raced down the cape in Gary's muscle car at speeds approaching 110. When they arrived at Gary's house, they were so scared they armed themselves with Uncle Shank's .12-gauge shotgun. They also called the county sheriff, who happened to be one of Gary's cousins. When deputies arrived, the boys told them they had heard a prowler, but the lawmen didn't stick around long. All the while Steven kept the shotgun at the ready.

"Damn, Stevie," said Dick Farrow, one of the deputies, "put that damn thing away."

"I can't. There's a man trying to break into this house."

"Look, Dick," Gary interrupted. "There's a guy in a Blazer who has been driving up and down the road. He got out and walked around the house. I ain't sure if he's trying to break in, but Stevie insisted I call the office and tell you all."

"Okay. What did the guy look like?"

"I ain't sure," said Gary.

"I am," said Steven. "He's got blond curly hair, about 29 years old and fat. The Blazer is a 1972, yellow with a black top."

"Okay, I'll check around and see if I can find him," said the deputy. "But Stevie, you need to get rid of that gun. Gary, take it from him and put it up before someone gets hurt."

"Somebody's going to get hurt if they come in that damn door without permission," said Steven.

"I think you both are overreacting, but I'll check it out," said the deputy, heading back to his car.

"Thanks, Dick," said Gary. "I'll get Stevie to put the gun up."

That night, Steven slept with his uncle's shotgun by his side. The incident had scared the hell out of him, but it had also excited him. Steven Russell had gotten his first big time adrenaline buzz; the rush that comes from chase. And he liked it.

After his graduation from Tidewater in the spring of 1976, Russell followed in the path established by his grandfather, his father, and his brother and began working full-time at the family produce business. Privately, however, he hoped to become a police officer—primarily to develop the skills that would help him track down his biological parents. He frequently visited the offices of various law enforcement agencies around the area, always making sure to drop off a basket of fruit or a box of vegetables at the same time.

During one such visit to the office of Norfolk's police chief, Charlie Grant, Russell met Debbie Davis, the chief's secretary. Like most of the girls he had dated in high school, she was petite, slightly older than Russell, and had long dark hair that tumbled down the entire length of her back. Davis belonged to the fundamentalist Church of God, and she wasn't interested in dating a nonmember. After about a month of being asked, and after getting a favorable recommendation for Russell from Chief Grant, she accepted one of Russell's invitations. Russell recalls the exact day of their first date, and exactly where they went: on March 15, 1975, he took her to dinner at Burroughs Bel Air Steak House on Military Highway in Norfolk. In the months that followed, they'd go to many other restaurants, to amusement parks, or on trips back to North Carolina, her home state, to visit her parents, three brothers, and three sisters. They rarely went to see movies, since Davis considered most of them sinful. Ditto for dancing, drinking, and premarital sex.

In August 1976, after 17 months of chaste courtship, Russell and Davis were married. About 500 people, including some 100 police officers, attended the wedding.

The ceremony featured two of the couple's favorite songs, "We've Only Just Begun" and "The Wedding Song." Russell's father was best man. Chief Grant drove Russell to the wedding. The couple honeymooned in Orlando, where they both lost their virginity. Upon their return, they settled into the house in Virginia Beach where Steven had grown up, vacant since his parents had moved into a nearby luxury condominium in a high-rise, the Cape Henry Towers, with a beautiful view of the Chesapeake Bay waterfront.

On the surface, at least, the Russells' was an old-school sort of marriage. Steven's weekdays began at 5 A.M. After a shave and shower, he'd grab a soda—he never drinks coffee or smokes—and read the newspaper. When he left in his four-wheel drive Dodge an hour later, Debbie would still be in bed. Debbie got off work from the police department at 4:30 P.M., and returned home to cook dinner. She also tended to the housework and cleaning. An employee from the produce business took care of the yard.

"I was really a lazy ass in those days," Russell says. "But Debbie would get mad at me if I tried to cook or clean. She was real traditional that way. Our home was spotless."

On weeknights, they usually stayed home and watched television, and retired no later than ten. Since both newlyweds liked to fish, they spent every weekend possible on the water in their 24-foot Sea Ray motorboat. Steven

even taught Debbie to clean her own catch. They both enjoyed cooking, and, despite Debbie's objections to him being in the kitchen, Russell taught her to make his favorite dishes, shrimp dumplings and blood rare steak. They were also Washington Redskins fans, and often drove five hours in Debbie's silver Lincoln Mark IV to RFK Stadium for football games. Other weekends, Debbie would sit and listen for hours while Steven played the organ they purchased for their home.

Compromising on the issue of religion, they joined the First Baptist Church of Norfolk. After church, on the Sundays they weren't at RFK, they'd usually drive to Debbie's mother's house in North Carolina for lunch. On Wednesdays Steven and Debbie often went with Chief Grant to the weekly Law Enforcement Officers Fellowship gatherings at Calvary Temple. And though Grant and his wife were many years older, the two couples became close friends. For four or five years, they frequently dined together, at home or out. When Grant's daughter got married, Russell played the organ at the service.

It seemed an idyllic life, and Steven was generally happy. He loved Debbie and had no interest in other women.

"I was in love and lust with Debbie," says Russell. "Deb was very pretty. Her long brown hair went down her back, and she only weighed about 100 pounds."

He adds that, at the time, he enjoyed sex with his wife as much as men today would "enjoy sex with Julia Roberts." However, he couldn't bring himself to tell Debbie that he was also sexually interested in men when he married her.

"I was attracted to guys at the same time," says Russell. "So, I guess I probably met the definition of bisexual. But I repressed those feelings of attraction towards guys."

He had convinced himself that his liaisons with men had been merely a phase, and now that phase was finished. And in the span of one year, he was about to enter two new phases of his life.

In 1979, Debbie gave birth to a daughter, Stephanie. Steven immediately became infatuated with her. Over Debbie's protests, he bought a tiny white poodle named Buffy for her. Thus began a special bond between father and daughter. Debbie served as enforcer and disciplinarian to Stephanie; Steven could not bring himself to spank her. As the child grew, without Debbie's knowledge Steven occasionally wrote notes granting his daughter permission to miss school whenever the two of them decided she needed a respite. Steven also made sure to speak with his daughter in detail about sex, boys and life in general—the heart-to-heart talks he felt he had never received from his own parents.

That same year, Russell became a police officer when

he joined the ranks of the Currituck County Sheriff's Office, just across the state line in North Carolina, as an unpaid part-time deputy, but a deputy nevertheless. To support his growing family, he also continued to work full-time at D. S. Russell & Sons.

While serving as a Currituck County deputy, Russell insists, he was a good, honest lawman. He took special pride in stopping speeders and getting drunk drivers off the road. Grant confirms that Russell had a good reputation; if anything, he says, Russell might have been a bit overzealous.

"I had a guy tell me that Steve stopped him once and told him he was going to write him a ticket," Grant says. "They weren't even in Steve's jurisdiction."

Russell volunteered his time largely due to his interest in learning investigative skills that he hoped would help him track down his biological parents. On the job, he focused on learning the intricacies of two policing tools: the National Law Enforcement Telecommunications Service (NLETS) and the National Crime Information Center (NCIC). NLETS, an Arizona-based nonprofit organization, is a computerized messaging network that enables the secure exchange of information between federal, state, and local law-enforcement agencies. NCIC, operated by the Federal Bureau of Investigation, is a data bank of criminal histories, physical descriptions, fingerprints,

Social Security numbers, aliases, and more—an invaluable tool for law officers nationwide.

His studies paid off quickly. When he initiated his first computer search, he had only his mother's name, Brenda Assaid Basham, which Georgia Russell had reluctantly provided years before. Within 20 minutes of running her name through the databases, Steven hit on a Brenda Basham in nearby Hampton, Virginia. Continuing his search, he learned that Brenda had been married to Thomas Carlyle Basham, that they had divorced and then remarried each other, and that his biological father was dead. The records also revealed that Brenda had given birth to two other boys, one older and one younger than Steven, and that neither of them had been given up for adoption.

"Since I had all of their DOBs [dates of birth] and Social Security numbers," he says, "I ran their credit histories and invaded the hell out of their privacy so I could try to understand how everything happened."

With the databases exhausted and questions lingering, Russell drove to Hampton. After a lot of indecision and driving around, he mustered his nerve, got out of his car, walked up to the front door of Brenda Basham's house, and knocked. When he identified himself and explained his reason for wanting to meet her—she was his mother—Basham denied it all, and dispatched Russell in short order. She didn't even invite him in.

As he drove away, dejected, Russell decided to bury his hope of uniting with the family he had never known. This conviction wouldn't last. Within a year, he would again try to connect with his blood relatives. In 1980, while visiting family in Elizabeth City, he dropped by the Pasquotank County Clerk's office, where he located his original birth certificate. Unlike the doctored certificate that David and Georgia Russell had, the original listed his real name as Steven Jay Basham. It also listed Brenda Assaid and Thomas Carlyle Basham as his parents, confirmation of his earlier investigation.

"But I was still too scared to confront Brenda again," he says. Instead, he decided to hang on to the document until the day when he would find the courage to knock on his mother's door again. A decade would pass before that day arrived.

In the late 1970s and early 1980s, Russell had plenty of other business to tend to. By that time, D. S. Russell & Sons was one of three dominant produce companies in Tidewater Virginia. At the time, area school districts ranked as some of the region's largest buyers of produce, along with many supermarket commissaries connected to the massive federal military bases in and around Norfolk.

For years, Russell & Sons only bid on orders from the school districts. Each week, David Russell met with representatives of the other two local companies, Tidewater Produce and Peninsula Produce, both based in Hampton, to discuss pricing. In truth, they were setting prices at certain levels to ensure that their companies, and only their companies, won the lucrative school contracts. This illegal practice, known as bid-rigging, continued unfettered until 1976. That year, shortly after Steven graduated from high school, his father had asked him to take over the family's contract bidding, and to sit in on the meetings with the company's two competitors.

Russell was only 18 at the time, but he raised the stakes. He demanded that the other two companies allow Russell & Sons not only to help set the school-district prices, but to join in the bidding for the military commissaries as well. Initially, the officials from the other two companies—Joseph and Matthew Russo from Tidewater and Robert Wright from Peninsula—balked at the idea of letting a punk like Steven have a cut of their deal. But Russell convinced his father that they should play hardball, crippling Tidewater and Peninsula by underbidding them for the military contracts. His father agreed.

To keep from attracting government attention, the Russells used a third party, a smaller produce wholesaler already involved in bidding on federal contracts, as a front. That company would make the bids and deliver the goods to the bases, using the Russells' ample credit

and warehouse space to undercut the other two companies. The Russells and the smaller company would then
split the profits down the middle.

The following week, the Russells and their new partner won almost every military produce contract up for
bid. Their rivals were furious. At their regular meeting
the next week with Steven, the Russos and Wright cursed
and screamed at him for an hour.

"Hell, I was only eighteen years old, and I didn't know
antitrust from shinola," Russell says. "But I wasn't going
to let them bully me and tell me who my family could or
couldn't sell to." After three weeks of being undercut, the
rival companies grudgingly agreed to let the Russells in
on the illegal weekly meetings to set prices for the military commissaries.

For several years, the arrangement worked fine. Then,
in 1980, prosecutors from the Department of Justice subpoenaed all three Russells—David, Steven, and his
brother Scott. When Steven and David were called to testify before a federal grand jury, Steven turned to his old
friend Reverend Sentell for advice. Cooperate with the
feds, Sentell told him. So Steven had the family's attorney
approach the prosecutors with an offer to assist them in
their investigation—a sting operation that locally became
known as Fruitscam.

It was easier than Steven had imagined. Even after getting subpoenaed themselves, the Russos and Wright were still greedy enough to want to talk about fixing prices. With tape recorders and video cameras rolling, Russell met with his counterparts and led them through a discussion of how much the school districts and military bases would pay for their next orders.

"We had our little bid-rigging session, and these guys were cussing like sailors while I just sat there and smiled," he says.

Soon, the government issued indictments against officials with five Tidewater produce companies for conspiring to illegally inflate the price of produce between 1975 and 1981. By the end of 1983, most of the defendants had pled either guilty or no-contest to the charges, and received short jail sentences and fines of $15,000 to $125,000. Steven's father pled guilty to conspiring to rig bids, his company pled guilty to two other conspiracy counts, and he agreed to testify against the other co-conspirators. In return, he received a probated sentence and a $15,000 fine.

The fact that Steven Russell himself was never indicted or charged in the investigation gave rise to speculation at the time by some in Norfolk, including Reverend Sentell and Chief Grant, that Steven had ratted out his father to save his own skin. Russell denies it. But toward the end of Fruitscam, he says, he began to worry about his future. He could clearly see that the family business was in trouble. And he assumed that, in the aftermath of the scandal that was becoming well-known throughout the industry, he had little future in the produce business.

Russell also feared that his life was in danger, or at least that's what he told Charlie Grant. So when Russell said he wanted to go to Florida, Grant felt compelled to help him. He told Russell he knew of a job opening with the police department in Boca Raton. Grant was friendly with the chief down there, and helped grease the skids for his young protégé. Steven Russell was about to become an honest-to-God officer of the law.

chapter five

Boca and Back

It didn't take long for trouble to find Steven Russell in Florida.

Frank Carey, the Boca Raton police chief, had recently worked in Norfolk as a crime analyst for Charlie Grant, and had also attended Reverend Sentell's Calvary Temple Church. Both Sentell and Grant contacted Carey on Steven Russell's behalf. Carey told them that if Russell graduated from the police academy, he would hire him. The Russells sold their Dodge and Lincoln, bought a 1980 Datsun station wagon, and headed south.

Soon after graduating from the police academy in November 1981, Russell was assigned to the department's traffic division. He was back to writing tickets and cuffing intoxicated drivers, his favorite policing duties back in North Carolina.

"I had seen how much damage a drunk driver could do to a family in my early years in law enforcement," he says. "I once had to tell a mother that her sixteen-year-old son was killed by a drunk driver. I'll never forget how hard that was. It was a moral thing with me, and I was good at it." For about ten months, things went well. Russell worked the traffic beat Tuesday through Saturday, 7:00 P.M. to 3:00 A.M., prime time for busting drunks. He racked up large numbers of DWI arrests, wrote many tickets, and even apprehended four suspects in a shopping mall armed robbery—while off duty, no less.

Although Debbie hated being so far from family and friends, Steven began to feel comfortable in his new life and surroundings, and he took to wearing pullover cotton shirts and khaki slacks. Located on Florida's Atlantic coast, Boca Raton seemed like a warmer and ritzier version of Virginia Beach, with all the fishing and water sports Russell had enjoyed back home, and palm trees to boot. For a more cosmopolitan atmosphere, Miami was only 45 miles south. If it wasn't quite paradise, it was awfully close, especially on a policeman's salary.

Like Russell, Chief Carey enjoyed driving around at night, talking on the police radio and making traffic stops.

Unlike Russell, Carey had not gone to school and been certified to operate a radar gun. Under Florida law, only a certified officer can issue speeding tickets, a detail the chief
chose to ignore. Carey allegedly tried to get around the law
by signing Russell's name to the citations he issued. Russell
became aware of Carey's unethical activity but remained
quiet out of loyalty, for a while. Then, somewhere along the
line, Carey learned of Russell's trouble in the produce business, and unexpectedly ordered Russell to take a polygraph
regarding his role the price-fixing scandal back in Virginia.
Russell passed the lie-detector test and the chief took no
action against him. Russell assumed he could relax.

But on November 2, 1982, Russell's one-year anniver-
sary with the police department, Carey abruptly fired
Russell from the force. The official reason given for his
sudden termination was for his calling in sick to his job
with the Boca Raton PD earlier that year to secretly
attend the highway patrol academy—where he was also
trying to get a job. However, after one day at the school,
Russell became homesick for Boca Raton, and returned
to the police department there.

"To this day, I don't know why Frank turned on me,"
Russell says, ignoring the fact that he had briefly been
AWOL.

But even Russell's co-worker, Sergeant Nick Calise, currently with the West Palm Beach County Sheriff's Depart-

ment, believes Carey's dismissal of Russell was excessive. In 1982, Calise worked for the Boca Raton Police Department, and often found himself alongside fellow officer Steve Russell, and he gives Russell high marks as police officer.

"He excelled in traffic accident investigations," says Calise.

In fact, Calise says Russell showed such an aptitude for the work of the traffic division, he was permanently assigned to the unit despite being a rookie. In most cases, says Calise, a rookie will rotate through all the divisions of a police department in order to develop overall skills as an officer. But in Russell's case, the traffic division seemed to be his natural calling.

"He and I were probably the leading two officers in the DUI [driving under the influence] enforcement we had going on back in those days."

Calise adds that he was stunned when, years later, he learned of some of the darker aspects of Russell's life, insisting those traits were simply not present in the Steven Russell he knew in Boca Raton. Nor, he says, can he explain the disintegration of the relationship between Russell and Chief Carey. (My attempts to locate Carey were unsuccessful.)

"I got the impression that there was something more going on between Steve's family and Frank Carey," says Calise.

Whatever happened, Steven and Debbie were left shocked, angry, and without many options. So they did what many other young parents in a jam do: They packed their things and headed back home to their families. But Steven also planned to get even. After leaving Florida, he stayed in contact with officers in Boca Raton who were disgruntled with Chief Carey's running of the department. He even returned to Florida to attend one of their gripe sessions. At the gathering, he told his former colleagues about Carey's habit of writing tickets with Russell's name forged on them.

The radar gun was the smoking gun the officers were looking for. A senior officer took Russell's information to the district attorney, and pressure began to mount for Carey to resign. The chief did not go quietly. When the DA's office convened a public hearing to sort out the facts, Chief Grant and Reverend Sentell urged Russell to retract his charges against Carey. Russell refused.

"I couldn't recant the charges against Frank," he says. "He did make those traffic stops, and I was not the radar operator. I felt absolutely horrible about [what he had done]. In those days, I took my job very seriously. I didn't cut any corners whatsoever, and I was an honest cop who didn't lie for anyone."

Soon after the hearing, Grant and Russell met for lunch in Norfolk.

"He took me to Tony's Hot Dogs for our last meal," Russell says. "After I refused to help, Charlie would have nothing more to do with me."

Twenty years later, what he sees as Russell's betrayal of Frank Carey still disturbs Grant, who is now retired.

"I took vacation time to go down to Florida for that hearing," he says. "Steve saw me and immediately left, and didn't even appear at the hearing. Because he knew I was going to tell them that he was the biggest liar who ever walked."

Despite that episode and all that has happened since, both Grant and Reverend Sentell admit that they still have mostly fond recollections of Russell. When I met with the two of them over a lunch of blueberry waffles at an International House of Pancakes near Sentell's church in Norfolk, even as they dished dirt on Russell, both men seemed compelled to defend and praise him as well.

"If you were to put him up against any fellow his own age [as a young man], characterwise and everything else, he'd be number one in my book," said Sentell.

"He'd be head and shoulders above them," said Grant.

"Yes, sir," said Sentell. "Because he was a kind-hearted human. Heart as big as a washtub. And I'm serious about it. He would come to me and say, 'Pastor, do you need anything?' And I'd say, 'Steve, I don't need anything.' But here he'd come with a case of this or a case of that. And he didn't steal it, because it was his own. I could call him up right now, and he'd send his shoes to me. He was as good a fellow as I ever met."

"He would come down to the police station to see me and Debbie," added Grant, "and he'd bring a watermelon or a basket of fruit."

"Big heart," Sentell reaffirmed. "Yes, sir. The man had a big heart."

Russell denies that he set up Carey. He is also adamant that, during his time in Boca Raton, he never acted on his homosexual desires. Absolutely no misbehaving whatsoever, he says. Nothing more than innocent men-watching during his idle time.

Back home in the secure surroundings of Norfolk, Russell resumed his old habit of driving around town in search of anonymous gay sex. Why, he can't say. "I had thought my desire for men was something that I could repress," he says. "But it didn't work that way."

He also thinks Charlie Grant may have been looking to get even with him. He believes Grant was so upset that the chief had undercover policemen place him under surveillance.

"Debbie is an all-round fine lady," says Grant of his former secretary. "She's a smart person and was a good secretary. But [Steven] could out-talk people, and he could always sell her on the idea that he didn't do what he was accused of. I'm sorry she ever got involved with him."

Wayside Park, on Military Highway, was one of Russell's favorite pick-up spots. In 1983, Russell was tooling through Wayside when he spotted a man sitting behind the wheel of a yellow taxi parked on the roadside. Russell parked, got out, and walked toward the cab. After strolling by several times, he stopped and looked in the window. The driver invited him to sit down. Russell did.

"I've never seen anyone come to the park in a cab before," he said to the cabbie.

"Well, I'm working, and I had a few minutes to take a break," the driver said. "I decided to come over here and see what was going on."

"That's cool," said Russell.

"So what are you looking to do this afternoon?" the driver asked.

"I'm open to almost anything," Russell replied.

"Can't you be a little more specific?"

"I'm open to almost anything," Russell repeated.

"Do you have a place to go?"

"Sure, we can go to the motel down Military Highway in Virginia Beach."

"I really don't have that much time."

"Well, I'm open to anything you suggest."

"Well, I'm cool to anything," said the driver. "What do you want from me?"

"A B.J.," Russell answered.

As soon as the words left Russell's mouth, the faux cab-driver flashed his Norfolk P.D. badge and arrested Russell for misdemeanor solicitation. Opting to challenge the arrest, Russell hired Virginia Beach attorney Dick Bridges. Bridges told his client not to worry. Through the luck of the judicial draw, Russell's case got assigned to the court of Judge Reid Spencer, who just a couple of years earlier, when he was still a defense attorney, had represented Russell and his father during the Fruitscam investigation. Spencer recused himself and transferred the case to the court of Judge Bert Saks, who had been a classmate of Bridges in law school.

During the trial, Bridges asked the undercover officer who had arrested Russell if the letters "B.J." were part of the alphabet. When the officer said yes, Bridges immediately requested that the case be dismissed. Judge Saks granted the request, and ordered Russell's arrest expunged from the records. No one in Russell's family or circle of friends found out about the incident.

Despite his close call, Russell continued to frequent the parks and restrooms of Norfolk. In May 1984, he picked up a hitchhiker on Ocean View Boulevard. Although the man seemed nervous, Russell was confident and unconcerned.

"I didn't think he was a cop," he says, "because he was too sissy-acting."

After the hitchhiker got in the car, Russell tried to let him do the suggesting, but the man didn't seem much of a conversationalist. Finally, Russell told the fellow the same thing he had said to the undercover officer: He wanted a B.J. The passenger told Russell to be patient, and that he needed to make a phone call. Russell drove him to a pay phone. After making the call, the stranger asked Russell to drop him back off on Ocean View. Russell figured the man had gotten cold feet, and that that was the end of the story.

A month later, Russell was engaging in oral sex with a man in a wooded area of Wayside Park when he noticed an approaching unmarked police car. The vehicle stopped, and three cops got out. Russell recognized one of them as the skittish male hitchhiker he had picked up a few weeks earlier. When the officers began approaching, Russell decided a hasty exit was in order. He made it to his car and got away, thankful he had apparently once again dodged a bullet.

In September, Norfolk police detectives arrested Russell while he was doing produce-related work in Virginia Beach. He was charged with solicitation for immoral purposes, frequenting a place or park for immoral purposes, and, in connection with his rapid departure from the Wayside Park three months earlier, reckless driving.

Again, Russell fought the charges. And again, the case was assigned to the court of Judge Spencer, who once again recused himself and transferred the case to Judge Saks. Saks ruled that the officers had failed to prove where the alleged offenses had occurred. The charges against Russell were dismissed and his record expunged. Afterward, Russell's attorney strongly encouraged him to stay out of public restrooms and parks unless he was there for conventional purposes. For a change, Russell heeded someone's advice.

"I stopped going to the park, and started dating guys," he says, adding that he did so without his wife's knowledge.

By 1983, because of the price-fixing scandal's aftereffects and losses in the company's trucking division, the Russell family produce business, where Steven had returned to work after his stint in Florida, was in a financial bind. Soon the firm had to file for bankruptcy and put its headquarters up for sale. In June, a former competitor named Art Sandler bought the company but retained Russell as an employee. Russell soon quit, intending to return to law enforcement.

Applying for a job with the sheriff's office in nearby Suffolk County, Russell managed to pass a polygraph test even though, in the process, he claimed he had never gotten arrested. Two weeks later, he got fired when his arrest for solicitation was uncovered. His past was starting to be unavoidable.

"Someone from Suffolk was telling some of our officers that they had hired this real crackerjack policeman named Steven Russell," says Charlie Grant. "And our guys told them they'd better get rid of him, and I think they fired him the next day."

Following the demise of the family business, Steven's father, David, grew despondent, and his health declined. Two years after the sale of the company, the elder Russell died of a heart attack in a North Carolina hotel. Georgia Russell was with her husband when he passed away. Some 500 mourners attended the funeral.

Steven Russell received the news that his father was gone in a 6:00 A.M. phone call from his brother, Scott, who had been dealing with his own personal demons. It was a turning point in the lives of both men.

"Right after Daddy's death, my brother straightened up and has never messed up since," Russell says proudly. He cannot say the same for himself.

chapter six

Coming Out
in Houston

Shortly after his abrupt and embarrassing dismissal from the Suffolk County Sheriff's Office, Russell returned to the industry he knew best. He landed a job with Sysco, a national food distributor, as director of produce operations. This meant relocating to the company's headquarters in Houston, a wondrous new world, especially for a man about to come to terms with his long-secret homosexuality.

While working for Sandler, Russell had been paid about $36,000 a year. Sysco doubled that salary. He used some of his new wherewithal to purchase a $175,000 house under construction in Northgate Forest, one of the dozens of upscale subdivisions, some with their own country club, that sprang up in Houston's suburbs in the 1980s. While he started his new job, Debbie and Stephanie stayed behind in Virginia.

While the house was being completed, Russell settled into a small apartment about fifteen miles north of downtown. There, he quickly discovered the differences between Houston and the Tidewater of Virginia. Virginia has more in common with conservative Dallas, which is sometimes called the Buckle of the Bible Belt. Houston, on the other hand, views itself as a city of wildcatters; a city that welcomes anyone with enough gall and talent to make a run at the brass ring. This wide-open business climate makes Houston a popular destination for grifters and con artists of the highest order. It's no coincidence that the recent Enron debacle, as well as many of the savings and loan failures of the late 1980s, took place there.

At the same time, few would describe Houston as a hotbed of liberalism. At more than 500 square miles, the city takes up most of Harris County, which annually sends more convicts to Death Row than most states. But that ultraconservative, eye-for-an-eye sense of justice coexists with more topless bars per capita than any other U.S. city. The unofficial civic motto seems to be, "Have a good time; just don't kill anyone while you're at it."

Unencumbered by his wife and child, he began sampling the city's pleasures. They were like nothing he'd ever known. Among other things, Houston offered a ballet, a symphony, and an opera—the fine arts that Russell loved but had never had much access to. He also became a diehard fan of Houston Rockets basketball. Russell also quickly discovered that the nation's fourth-largest city also has a significant gay population. He began attending Bering Memorial United Methodist Church, which gears its ministry to gays and lesbians. ("I still consider myself a religious man," he says. "My beliefs are the same as a Methodist, but including homosexuality.") Above all, he found himself drawn to the city's Montrose area.

According to a spokesman for the Houston Gay and Lesbian Political Caucus, about 7,200 gay men and lesbians live in Montrose, making it the country's third largest primarily gay residential neighborhood.

"Being shy wasn't a problem for me once I hit Houston," he says. "Hell, if they were cute and had personality, I'd ask anyone out on a date. I was rarely attracted to professional people. I like the artsy types; the people who can do things I can't do."

During his trips into Montrose, Russell always made sure to use a false name with his new acquaintances. Most of his under-the-radar relationships during that time might be described as hit-and-runs. He refuses to reveal the name he used there, or the names of the numerous male sexual conquests he claims. He maintains, however, that they included a Rice University professor, a concert pianist, and numerous other musicians. He has remained in touch with a few of them, he says. Many others have died of AIDS. Russell has no idea how he managed not to become infected with HIV himself.

"I once learned that a guy I was dating was HIV-positive, and I just freaked out," he says. "He and I were camped out at the Four Seasons. He was my third serious lover since I'd moved to Houston. Anyway, while we were at the hotel, I began to notice that he took a lot of medication. So when he wasn't looking, I wrote down the name of one of the prescription drugs he was taking, Retrovein, and snuck off and called a pharmacy to find out what it was for. They told me Retrovein was AZT, one of the anti-AIDS drugs. I freaked out! He died the next year."

Most of the men Russell met during this time seemed more sophisticated than him and most people he had known back in Virginia. Two of them sold clothes at Sakowitz, a now-defunct department store. They taught Russell how to dress, he says. Before moving to Houston, he had worn store-brand suits; his salesmen friends introduced him to designer labels such as Giorgio Armani. They coached him about his table manners. He was exposed to fine wine and gourmet food, and was invited to elaborate dinner parties.

"Most of my dates didn't materialize into anything serious," says Russell. "For one thing, I was still married. But I was beginning to accept my sexuality and who I was, and not be ashamed of it. I was beginning to enjoy the lifestyle, and I was becoming less and less concerned about who knew."

With the notable exceptions, that is, of his wife and his daughter. In January 1985, Debbie and Stephanie joined Steven in Houston, and the three of them moved into their new house on Blackcastle Court. This reunion put a crimp in Russell's new lifestyle.

"Before Debbie and Stephanie moved to Houston, I spent all my free time dating," he says. "After they came, I only spent half my free time dating."

Debbie liked Houston even less than Boca Raton. In January, it was still too hot. She missed Virginia, missed the change of the seasons, and missed her family. She loathed Houston's traffic, and the city's high violent crime rate frightened her. The local news seemed to feature almost daily reports of someone getting blown away or hacked to death over some drug deal gone bad. She hated the almost-caricatured brashness of some of her neighbors. Debbie remained deeply religious, and she felt she had little in common with big-haired Houston housewives who hung out at the country club golfing and knocking back cocktails in the middle of the afternoon. In Houston, she had no job and felt she had no identity. With Stephanie in school, she had little more to do all day than walk around their big new house. Her exile would last just over two years.

The evening of April 15, 1986, began as many of Steven's evenings did. He picked up one of his new male friends, one of the clothing salesmen from Sakowitz, for dinner in his new Corvette, and drove into the city. They ate dinner, then went dancing at a bar in Montrose. Late that evening they returned to the salesman's apartment. About an hour and a half later, Russell dressed, got into his car, and began driving home to his wife and daughter on the city's far north side. He was feeling good. He'd just romanced a handsome young man. The wine at dinner and cocktails at the bar had left him with a pleasant glow. Now he sat behind the wheel of a high-performance sports car. How could things get any better?

Making his way home, he was driving the Corvette north on Gessner Road, doing about 60 in a 35-mile-per-hour zone, when he passed an oncoming patrol car. The police car braked and quickly whipped around. Russell stomped on the Corvette's accelerator. As he approached a set of railroad tracks, he lost control of the car.

"The Corvette hit the tracks sideways," he says, "and flipped over seven or eight times, throwing me through the canvas top and into a ditch full of water."

Russell's pelvis was flattened, broken in three places. At the hospital, he was given at least 15 pints of blood to stabilize him. During his eight weeks in the intensive care unit at Spring Branch Memorial Hospital, doctors expected him to die from either liver or kidney failure. Somehow he survived. His marriage, however, did not.

In the wake of the accident, Debbie had plenty to do. In addition to commuting between north Houston and the hospital on the west side of town, she took over the family's finances. As she sorted through the monthly bills, she noticed that their credit card statement included stays in various hotels. Assuming her husband had been seeing other women, she confronted him. Russell denied her accusations.

"I told her they were for prospective job applicants coming to interview with Sysco from out of state," he says. Russell doesn't think Debbie believed him, but she didn't push the matter any further then. She paid the bill and continued to nurse him back to health.

By December 1986, Russell was capable of taking care of himself. Without drama or further accusations, Debbie packed up her belongings and her seven-year-old daughter and headed back to Virginia. Before they left, Russell decided it was finally time to be completely honest with Debbie about his secret sexuality. He can't recall exactly how the conversation went. (Debbie refuses to discuss it.) He just remembers that after it was over, both of them seemed to be relieved.

"She handled the situation with class and was nonconfrontational," Russell says. "She wanted to go back to Chesapeake, and I encouraged her. But Debbie is the finest woman a man could ever have in his life. I can't stress enough how strongly I feel about how great a person Deb is."

As Debbie was preparing to leave, Russell resigned from Sysco to head up the corporate produce division of one of its competitors, White Swan Foods. Two years later, White Swan promoted him to executive vice president of sales, marketing, and merchandising. Not long after, White Swan officials let Russell in on a secret of their own: They had just negotiated a deal with their two main competitors, Sysco and Glazier Foods, to fix the prices of produce sold to 22 Houston-area school districts.

"So I'm thinking, this is just great," Russell says. "I was still trying to forget about the bid-rigging mess back in Virginia, and now here it was again. Remember, this was 1988. At this point, I still didn't have any convictions, and I was trying to live a crime-free life. These guys were getting greedy, and the brokers who work the Houston market were not exactly stupid. They know what's going on, and they were bound to find out."

To avoid getting entangled in another federal investigation, in early 1989 Russell contacted Peter Goldberg, the assistant U.S. attorney who had overseen the Fruitscam investigation back in Virginia.

"Goldberg told me he would contact the appropriate [federal] personnel," Russell says. "I began looking for another job."

Russell applied for a job in Los Angeles with S.E. Rycoff & Co., a produce distribution company with 23 branches and $2.7 billion in annual revenues. During the application process, he called Rycoff's director of human resources and claimed to be the chief financial officer of another company.

"I told the guy that I knew Steve Russell," he says, "and that he ought to talk to him. I said he was good employee prospect."

Three months later, Rycoff hired Russell as director of restaurant sales and assistant to the president of its Los Angeles division. In April 1989, Russell headed for California, certain that he was leaving another bidding scandal behind.

Two months later, another assistant U.S. attorney from the Justice Department's antitrust division contacted Russell. He wanted more information on the Houston bid-rigging allegations Russell had passed along, and he wanted Russell to help federal investigators, just as he had in Virginia. He asked Russell if he would once again be willing to wear a wire.

Reluctantly, Russell agreed. Months elapsed before the investigation kicked into high gear. In the meantime, he tried, in vain, to settle into his new job at Rykoff.

"It was a very conservative company, and everybody there was very set in their ways," he says. He also felt that his co-workers resented him. He set high sales goals for himself and expected the same from his staff.

"People in L.A. don't like to work hard," he says. "I do. I'm very intense. Rykoff was a laid-back company. That's why they got into financial trouble. They had the attitude that they were doing their customers a favor to sell to them; that's why their revenues declined. Their CEO didn't have the nuts to change that mindset."

It didn't help that at the same time Russell was also undergoing romantic and financial problems. Shortly after this, Russell began casually dating a male employee at Rykoff's office in Beverly Center.

"We didn't really hit it off," he says, "and he got pissed off when I cut him loose."

Out of spite, Russell says, the man mailed a note to Russell's boss, exposing Russell's homosexuality. The situation worsened when Rykoff began receiving calls from creditors back in Virginia, seeking to collect payments on debts that had never been resolved after the Russell family's produce business had collapsed. Concerned by the calls, Rykoff officials ran a background check on Russell. Their investigation revealed that the CFO who had called to recommend Russell did not really exist, and that Russell been arrested in Norfolk for indecent exposure—even though the arrest had supposedly been expunged.

In November 1989, Rykoff dismissed him. Russell returned to Norfolk, where for two months he camped out at Debbie's house. Although she had left him three years earlier, she still had not filed for divorce. Indeed, Debbie and Steven had remained close, and they were happy to spend Christmas together with their daughter, who was now ten.

Following the holidays, in January 1990, yet another produce distribution company, CONCO Foodservice of New Orleans, hired Russell to be chief operating officer of its office in Shreveport, Louisiana. Russell now used this new position to get his revenge. Before applying at CONCO, Russell had approached White Swan about possibly returning there. But White Swan officials had heard the sordid details of Russell's dismissal from Rykoff, and they turned him down.

"After I went to work for CONCO, I hired about thirteen of White Swan's seventeen Houston sales associates," he says proudly. "They all quit the same day, and started calling White Swan customers under the CONCO name on a beautiful sunny Monday morning in March."

Thus began a corporate civil war of sorts, according to Russell. Again, copies of his supposedly expunged arrest record from Norfolk surfaced suspiciously, and were sent to executives at CONCO. Although he didn't lose his job with CONCO right away, Russell called the Dallas office of the Justice Department's antitrust division and told them he suspected White Swan and Sysco were engaging in price fixing.

At the Justice Department's behest, beginning in February 1990, Russell held a series of meetings with executives from both White Swan and Sysco. He first met with Joe Mobley, Sysco's bid manager, at one of his old hangouts in Montrose, Felix's Mexican Restaurant, a neighborhood favorite. As the two men exchanged pleasantries and nibbled tortilla chips, Russell casually updated Mobley about his recuperation from his Corvette accident. Just as casually, he told Mobley that he wanted in on the school bid deal that Sysco had worked out with its two main competitors.

"Well, I don't have a problem dividing things up four ways," Mobley said, "but I'm sure my boss would."

"Could you talk to him and see what he thinks?" Russell asked. "I sure don't want to come in and take all this business and lowball all of you guys' bids."

"I've already talked to him," said Mobley. "He figured this was exactly why you set up this meeting."

"Has he turned psychic?"

"No, he just knows you're very competitive."

"Well, tell him what I want, and see if he will allow us to come in. My phone number's on the card. Call me if he agrees. Let's eat now."

"Okay," said Mobley. "But don't get mad if I don't call you."

In fact, Mobley never did call, and Russell never saw him again. But the FBI had recorded, videotaped, and photographed the conversation. Soon, a similar conversation, with a White Swan manager, took place at another Mexican restaurant, and it, too, was electronically documented.

By June 1990, four months after Russell began his little chats, word of the federal probe had leaked to the Houston media, and Justice Department officials confirmed it to the *Houston Chronicle*. In all, federal prosecutors claimed that profits from illegal bidding exceeded $16 million.

Almost four years later, federal records show that White Swan and Sysco each pled guilty to one charge of bid-rigging. Sysco was fined $2 million; White Swan $650,000. Additionally, Mobley, along with one executive from White Swan and one executive from Glazier Foods, was found guilty of bid-rigging and mail fraud, and they were eventually sentenced to five years' probation and four months of home confinement. According to Russell, it couldn't have happened to a more deserving bunch of guys.

"I don't have any regrets about dropping them in grease," he says. "I was trying to live right and be a law-abiding citizen during that time."

Of course, there may have been other motives at work.

"Let's put it this way," Russell says. "I never forget shit. I am not a good person to have as an enemy."

In addition, Russell had hoped to capitalize on Sysco and White Swan's legal problems to better position CONCO in the Houston market. But he never got the chance. Once reports of his indecent exposure arrest began to circulate through CONCO, his support from the company's managers evaporated. In May 1990, five months after starting there, he resigned.

"All the guys I helped put [away]," he muses, "they're probably laughing at me today."

chapter seven

A New Family
and a Life of Crime

In June 1990, Steven Russell returned yet again to Norfolk, where he did not exactly receive a hero's welcome. He was broke and without any resources, options, or friends who could rescue him from his predicament. The family business was no more than a memory. His father was dead, his mother had moved to Florida, and his brother had gone to Texas to start a new life. Most of his contacts in law enforcement had vanished along with his friendship with Charlie Grant. Russell remained on good terms with one old family friend, Sergeant Al Barbour of the Chesapeake Police Department. And Barbour introduced him to Lloyd Allen, a patrolman assigned to Chesapeake's traffic and radar division, Russell's former beat in Boca Raton.

The two men hit it off immediately. Allen, a man of medium build and thinning red hair, even invited Russell to ride shotgun on patrol with him. Russell gratefully accepted, and often tagged along with Lloyd.

"He drove and I assisted him," Russell says. "I was carrying my .357 nickel-plated Smith & Wesson. I wrote out tickets and Allen signed them. Hell, I even talked on the radio. Everybody knew me and it was tolerated."

Their friendship would lead to a startling meeting. One August night, Allen introduced Russell to the woman working dispatch at the Chesapeake police station. (Allen, now retired, confirms the meeting as well as his friendship with Russell.)

"Debbie, this is my unofficial partner, Steve Russell. Steve, this is our night shift dispatcher, Debbie Basham."

Basham—the name of Russell's birth mother.

"Basham," Russell repeated, trying to stay calm. "That's not a very common name."

"No, it's not," the dispatcher agreed.

Only the garbled tinny chatter from the police radios broke the awkward silence.

"I think I may be related to some Bashams," Russell finally volunteered.

"My husband's first name is Mitch," Debbie replied.

When he heard that name, Russell's pulse quickened again. During his searches for clues that he had hoped would lead him to his natural family years earlier, Russell had learned that Brenda Basham had a son named Thomas Mitchell Basham.

"I think you're my sister-in-law," Russell blurted out.

Sharing the excitement, Debbie Basham told Russell that her husband also had a younger brother named Mark, a radiologist who lived in Norfolk, as well as a younger sister. (Oddly, Russell can't remember her name.)

Debbie invited Russell to her house to meet her family that night. Despite his reluctance, remembering what a disaster his first attempt to contact Brenda Basham had been, he accepted. But first he armed himself by stopping off and picking up his birth certificate.

Russell need not have feared. The people who indeed turned out to be his brothers and his sister were friendly, and intrigued rather than upset by the prospect of suddenly having a new long-lost brother, one who shared such genetic traits as their distinctively bony fingers and rounded toes, features that Russell's daughter, Stephanie, also inherited. What interested them most was the revelation that their mother and father had divorced after the birth of their first child. Then, after giving up their second child, Steven, the couple had reunited and produced two more children. After some discussion, the siblings decided they had to confront their mother.

Since Steven's newfound sister lived only a few blocks from Brenda, they decided to reconvene the next day and then invite their mother over, without telling her why. The next day, after a few cocktails for courage, they called Brenda. She arrived a few minutes later.

"Mom, this is Steven Russell," Mark said as she sat down. "We've all got something to talk about. First, I'm going to let Debbie tell you how this all got started."

Debbie told about her encounter with Russell in the dispatch office, then handed her Russell's birth certificate. She scrutinized it closely.

"Well?" Mark asked after a few moments.

"I feel like you're all ganging up on me," Brenda said.

"No, we aren't," said Mark. "Look, it's not a big deal. Hell, he probably had an easier life away from us."

"I think it's cool we have a brother no one knew about but you," said Mitch. "But what happened?"

Brenda saw no choice but to come clean. "Your dad and I got divorced in 1957, and a few months later, Steven was born," she said. "We decided to give him up for adoption since we couldn't care for him financially."

"Does this mean that we're bastards?" asked Mark.

"Mark, you're such an asshole," Brenda shot back.

"No, I think this is all really neat," Mark said earnestly.

"We have a brother we never knew about, and you've been keeping this secret from us for over thirty years. That's really cool. I just think it's time we welcomed him into our family and started treating him like a brother."

"I agree," Brenda said.

"Me, too," said Russell's sister.

"Well, I'm sorry if Brenda got caught by surprise," said Russell. "That wasn't my intention. I already made that mistake once when you all lived in Hampton."

"Steven, I'm sorry," Brenda said, "but you caught me at a very bad time when you showed up."

"It's okay," said Russell. "We all make mistakes."

"Things will be different now," Brenda promised.

"That's right," said Mark. "Let's celebrate by having dinner."

Everyone agreed, and they brought along the family's photo albums, including pictures of the father and the grandparents Russell had never seen.

For a time after this reunion, Russell saw his siblings and his mother often. He visited their homes, and they came to his. They shared meals and stories. Russell celebrated Thanksgiving at Brenda's home with the family. For a short time, he enjoyed the kind of relationship with his natural family that he had long dreamed of.

⌒

Not long after completing his lifelong search for his origins, Russell began to pull away. He had found his birth family, but the rest of his life felt like a disaster. He had lost the adoptive family that had provided him with love and an income. After twice assisting federal agents to uncover price-fixing schemes, he was now, in his own mind at least, banned for life from the produce business. After his arrests for solicitation and his role in the ouster of Frank Carey as chief in Boca Raton, he could no longer turn to his onetime friend Charlie Grant for help. Not that it mattered. A law-enforcement career in any jurisdiction no longer seemed viable. At this point, Russell made a conscious decision to become a career criminal.

This transformation had begun in Houston shortly before he had returned to Virginia. In April 1990, to raise some cash in anticipation of his departure from CONCO, Russell had faked a slip-and-fall accident at the high-rise apartment that CONCO had temporarily rented for him.

"I supposedly fell in the stairwell in the garage," he says, "and was transported to Hermann Hospital, where I used my old back and pelvis injuries as the crux of my problem. It was a very impetuous decision."

After the hospital released him, Russell threatened legal action against the apartment complex. Home Insurance settled with him for $45,000. By December 1990, Russell needed more cash, so he sold his two Rolex watches.

Pleased with how easily he was able to find buyers, he figured selling watches might not be a bad interim business. Having none left to sell, he decided to steal one.

Through his friendships with Lloyd Allen and other policemen, Russell still had access to law enforcement databases, and to advance his plan, he decided to use them to steal someone else's identity. In fact, says Allen, the situation almost got him fired. Russell settled on Steven Lynde Russell, of Virginia Beach. Once he had obtained the other Steven Russell's Social Security number and date of birth, he opened a charge account at a Virginia Beach jewelry store, where he purchased two more Rolexes, which he immediately sold to another local jeweler for $6,000 apiece.

"I didn't even need a driver's license," he says. But he got one anyway—in Steven Lynde Russell's name. The clerk at the Department of Motor Vehicles office in Virginia Beach knew Russell; she was married to the police chief in Chesapeake. But she evidently didn't notice that the Russell standing in front of her bore no resemblance to the photograph of Steven Lynde Russell the agency had on file. With his new identification in hand, Russell bought an expensive computer on credit at a shop in Chesapeake, and then quickly sold it to a friend for $2,000.

Within a month or so, the real Steven Lynde Russell began receiving some puzzling bills in the mail, and he soon contacted the Virginia State Police. After a short investigation, Russell surrendered to the police and was sentenced to five years' probation. Around the same time, federal prosecutors in Houston were building a case against Russell on another matter. Before getting arrested in Virginia, Russell had visited a friend in Houston. There he had used the identity of yet another Steven Russell— Steven Joseph Russell—to apply for a passport under a false address. As his criminal enterprises expanded, he figured a fake passport might come in handy at some point.

A federal grand jury subsequently indicted Russell for passport fraud. When federal agents tracked him to his former address in Houston, they found out about his alleged accident there, and the insurance settlement that had resulted. Suspecting that Russell may have faked the fall, the agents notified the Harris County district attorney's office. That office launched its own investigation, and soon indicted Russell for felony insurance fraud. The eventual outcome: Russell was ordered to serve six months—the maximum under mandatory sentencing guidelines—in a federal correctional facility on the passport fraud charge.

In what was becoming typical fashion, he bonded out from all the charges and found temporary sanctuary at his adoptive mother Georgia Russell's new home in West Palm Beach, Florida. When the time arrived for him to begin serving his sentence at Great Plains Federal Correctional Center in Oklahoma City, he simply didn't show up.

Instead, surprisingly, he made his way back one more time into the produce business, this time specializing in tomatoes in for the Costco company in Florida. Being a tomato broker, Russell thinks, is probably his true calling in life. From the age of six, he had been groomed for it. He understands tomatoes intimately—their growing seasons, their growing methods, their diseases, their size. In fact, he is downright passionate about vine-ripened tomatoes, viewing with contempt those ripened by other methods. "I can't stand to eat anything but a vine-ripened tomato," he says. "I absolutely love them."

While brokering his beloved tomatoes, Russell felt a need to bend the rules. There are four grades of tomatoes: U.S. #1, U.S. #2, U.S. Combination, and U.S. #3. According to Russell, there are two keys to making a profit on tomatoes: First, you have to see the product up close. Second, you must buy lower-grade tomatoes and then sell them as higher-grade #1s.

Before purchasing a shipment, Russell would personally inspect the produce at the packing house. U.S. Department of Agriculture inspectors, he says, are prone to under-grade produce they see in the field. He would search for tomatoes that a farmer believed rated as Combination, the third-highest designation, but which

Russell believed were really #2 tomatoes—and which he could sell to stores at #1 prices. Most chain grocery store buyers have little experience with produce grades, he says.

"That's how you make money in the produce business," he explains. "It's called field/ground buying. It's a fast-paced business, and if you don't know what the fuck you're doing, you'll get burned."

As a corollary to that principle, if you do know what you're doing, you can burn someone else, which is precisely what Russell did. At one point he was clearing $4,000 to $6,000 a week. He only wished he had started on this angle sooner—for instance, before he began falsely using other people's names to obtain credit and passports.

Also during this tomato phase, for the first time in his life, Russell fell flat-out in love with another man. This was when he first saw James Kemple. In June 1991, Russell and a one-night stand were checking into the Four Seasons Ocean Grand Hotel in Palm Beach. Kemple, a bellhop, offered to show them to their room. The next day, while checking out of the hotel, Russell began flirting with Kemple. Kemple responded by giving Russell his phone number.

A week later, Russell called him, and the two men went out on a date. Russell wasn't particularly interested in a relationship; with legal problems raining down on him, he had enough to worry about. But Russell's difficulties paled in comparison to those of Kemple, who was 25, nine years younger than Russell, and HIV-positive. At that time, people viewed that as tantamount to a death sentence. To his credit, Kemple revealed his condition to Russell as soon as they began dating.

Born in 1966 and raised in King of Prussia, Pennsylvania, Kemple was the son of a divorced couple. His mother, Helen, worked as a technical assistant for Johnson & Johnson. His father, Charles, was a supervisor at a food processing plant. His sister, Kimmy, taught autistic children. After finishing high school, Kemple had attended Virginia Commonwealth University in Richmond, just thirty miles from where Russell had been sent to reform school as a boy. In 1990 he'd moved to West Palm Beach and supported himself by waiting tables at several different restaurants. By the time he and Russell met, he'd become a bellman and was earning about $35,000 a year.

The two men fell hard for each other, and soon Russell and Kemple were going out almost every night. The interests they shared read like a list in a personals ad: They both loved movies, eating out, attending concerts, puppies, travel, cooking. They saw two or three movies a week, and enjoyed both trendy Palm Beach restaurants and funkier places like Nathan's Hot Dogs. Both watched TV avidly. *Melrose Place* and *Law and Order* ranked among their favorites. They especially enjoyed Sunday mornings together in front of the tube, beginning with Charles Kuralt.

"Then we'd watch the political shows so we could bash the Republicans," Russell says.

In October 1991, after dating for a couple of months, the two men pooled their furniture and took a two-bedroom apartment in a complex on a golf course in West Palm Beach. In some striking ways, Russell's life with Kemple would be something of a preview of his life with Phillip Morris just a few years later. For example, as he did with Morris, Russell bought three miniature Doberman Pinschers, naming them Barney, Jake, and Jagger. Also similarly to his life with Morris, each morning Russell got up at 7:00 and made coffee for Kemple, who worked until 11:00 P.M. at the Four Seasons and usually slept in. Before leaving the apartment, Russell would also check the weather and market reports for the entire country that he received every morning via fax. He'd then begin his morning rounds of Costco stores in the area, checking the produce stock at each. At that point, he was buying about $100 million worth of produce a year for Costco.

"Costco's volume made D. S. Russell & Sons look like a 7-Eleven," he says.

After lunch, it was on to farms in Palmetto, Ruskin, Homestead, and Lantana to inspect tomatoes, and then to the citrus houses in Vero Beach and Winter Haven to buy grapefruit.

It was not a bad life. Costco paid him $50,000 a year to putter around the produce fields and warehouses in his 1990 Ford Bronco. On top of that, his freelance tomato brokering deals aside from Costco brought him about $200,000 annually. But his legal problems would not go just because he was in love and gainfully employed. A month after moving in with Kemple, he was sentenced to six months in prison on the passport fraud charge, though he was given a few months to get his affairs in order before reporting. Then, in March 1992, he was ordered to serve 90 days in jail in Chesapeake as part of his sentence for the jewelry and computer thefts since he had violated the terms of his probation by leaving Virginia without approval from his probation officer. He agonized over his looming imprisonment, sinking into a deep funk. A doctor he consulted diagnosed him as clinically depressed and prescribed Xanax. Russell began drinking heavily. He also kept his legal tangles secret from Kemple. Whenever he left Florida to appear in court in either Virginia or Houston, he told Kemple that the proceedings concerned his past cooperation with the government in its price-fixing investigations, or lingering problems with his prior employers.

In March 1992, on the night before Russell was scheduled to report to the federal prison in Oklahoma, he met Kemple for dinner at a Benihana in Fort Lauderdale. During the meal, Russell drank excessively. After dinner, the two agreed to meet back at their apartment since they'd arrived in separate cars. Russell dreaded both the thought of six months in prison and the thought of telling Kemple about his situation. He drove around instead, stewing over his fate and continuing to drink. He also swallowed about 35 Xanax tablets.

Somewhere along the way, he pulled his Jaguar into a convenience store parking lot and called his ex-wife Debbie to tell her goodbye. Although Debbie had recently divorced him, she and their daughter Stephanie had remained close to him. Despite her own conservative moral code, both she and Stephanie had inexplicably accepted Russell's gay lifestyle and his new life with Kemple. Russell was still a large force in the lives of Debbie and Stephanie. But now Russell's life was in jeopardy. During his conversation with Debbie the Xanax kicked in, and Russell collapsed in a heap on the pavement.

He awoke the next morning in a room at Holy Cross Hospital in Fort Lauderdale, where paramedics had rushed him to the emergency room. There to greet him were Debbie, Stephanie, Kemple, and a psychiatrist. The doctor began questioning Russell, who was less than cooperative.

"After you left the restaurant, where did you go?" asked the psychiatrist.

"Rode around Fort Lauderdale popping Xanax," Russell replied.

"How many did you take?"

"Somewhere between 90 and 120."

"What happened then?"

"I died and went to heaven."

"You're lucky to be alive."

"That's what you think," said Russell. He then explained how he had failed to report to prison.

"What's the name of the marshal you were supposed to report to, so I can call him and explain?" asked the doctor.

"None of your fucking business," said Russell. "Are you working for him or what?"

The psychiatrist told him he had a duty to report him to the authorities, and that he would seek a court order confining Russell to his hospital room. Russell had heard enough.

"I still had five or six hundred dollars in my pants," he says. "So I got dressed and took off out of the hospital, jumped in a cab, and headed home for West Palm Beach, with all of them trailing behind me."

In the traffic, Russell managed to elude his pursuers, so he had the cab driver stop at a Costco pharmacy. Sporting two black eyes from his fall the night before, he got his Xanax supply refilled. Pills in hand, he then had the cabbie drop him off at his apartment. This time, he gulped down the entire bottle of Xanax—100 of them—and lay down with one of his and Kemple's puppies. When Kemple arrived a short time later, he had the nearly unconscious Russell rushed by ambulance to St. Mary's Hospital in West Palm Beach, his second trip to an emergency room in less than 24 hours.

It took Russell several days to recover from this second overdose. This time he regained consciousness in the hospital's intensive care unit. Once again, Kemple, Debbie, and Stephanie were there, along with another psychiatrist, Dr. Alan Flagman. Russell now describes Flagman as the finest psychiatrist he ever met. He credits him, and the new prescription he wrote for him, with saving his life.

"Dr. Flagman and Prozac really helped me through a very tough time," he says.

After his release from intensive care, Russell spent fourteen days under observation in the hospital's psychiatric unit. When it came time for him to be discharged, he told Kemple he would meet him at home. Debbie was still there, and Kemple drove her back to the apartment in a car she had rented, leaving Russell's Jaguar at the hospital so he could drive himself home.

But during the discharge process, Russell took his time

leaving, and instead chatted and joked with the doctors and nurses as he signed a stack of forms and billing statements. Clearly, he was feeling almost like his normal self. Suddenly one doctor at the busy nurses' station managed to get his attention.

"You need to leave now," the doctor said, a sense of urgency in his voice.

Russell later found out that the judge who had sentenced him was not amused that Russell had failed to report to prison, and had ordered the FBI to arrest him. "The doctor warned me because of loyalty," Russell says. "He also didn't like being used by the police."

Russell didn't have to be told twice. He was on his way home when his beeper went off. Kemple had punched in the emergency code they had agreed upon, 911, which meant that the police were also at their house. Russell immediately changed course.

First, he drove to the Ritz-Carlton and checked into a room. Determined not to end up in jail, he sat down and tried to decide his next move, short of another suicide attempt. He called Kemple on his cell phone and told him to come to the hotel so they could work out a plan. When Kemple arrived, Debbie was with him. Neither was in a good mood. Since Russell's death no longer seemed imminent, Debbie announced that she and Stephanie were going back to Virginia. That was a good idea, Russell told her, and he suggested she keep a low profile. After Debbie and Stephanie left, Russell began outlining for Kemple his plan to go on the run.

Without any warning, the slightly built, sweet-tempered Kemple reared back and launched his right fist into Russell's jaw. The impact of the punch stunned Russell.

"That skinny fuck hurt me," he says. "He wanted me to go ahead and do the time, and then get out and come back home to him."

But Russell being Russell, he couldn't see the point of that. He stayed on at the hotel for days, drinking profusely and sliding back into depression. Within a week his suicidal urges resurfaced. His Xanax prescription had run out, so he chugged down his bottle of blood pressure pills.

This time he awoke in the intensive care unit of Good Samaritan Hospital in West Palm Beach, his third hospital after his third suicide attempt in three weeks. On hand to greet him when he woke up this time were both of the psychiatrists who had treated him after his previous suicide attempts, along with an unfamiliar new visitor: a female detective from the West Palm Beach police who didn't hesitate to serve Russell with a federal warrant for his arrest. A guard was posted at the door of his hospital room around the clock.

In just two years, Russell had transformed himself from a produce buyer and ex-policeman with no criminal record, a generous (if former) husband and doting father, to a federal fugitive charged with theft in Virginia, insurance fraud in Texas, and passport fraud by the U.S. government, averaging one suicide attempt per week.

After recovering from his third overdose, in April 1992 Russell was flown to Houston, escorted by a Harris County deputy, as a result of his previous failure to report to federal prison. Although he was to have reported to prison in Oklahoma, he had been ordered to prison by a federal judge in Houston, whom he would now have to face again. But at the time, federal authorities in Houston had limited space for prisoners, so the Department of Justice contracted with the Harris County sheriff's office to house federal prisoners in the county jail. Russell was taken to the facility at 1301 Franklin, where he didn't even get a mattress of his own.

But he wouldn't stay there long.

chapter eight

The First Escape

It's a long way down from the luxurious Ritz-Carlton Hotel just south of Palm Beach, Florida, where Steven Russell and James Kemple occasionally stayed, to the sometimes tubercular-infested air of Houston's Harris County Jail. In April 1992, some three years before he and Phillip Morris first crossed paths there, that's precisely where Russell found himself.

At the time, the jail was only ten years old, but it was already outdated due to overcrowding, despite the construction of a second downtown jail a few blocks away in 1987. Neither was a very inviting place to spend time. A study by the Texas Department of Health found that in

1991, 574 cases of tuberculosis were reported in the Harris County jails, a 7.8 percent increase from the previous year. The reason for the increase: chronic overcrowding.

In April 1992, when Russell entered the older jail at 1301 Franklin Street, most inmates slept on the floor; lucky ones got a mattress. Russell was not among the lucky. So he decided to make other arrangements. His boyfriend, Kemple, had been diagnosed as HIV-positive. Neither he nor Russell knew how much time together they had left. Russell had no intention of stewing in prison while Kemple's condition worsened.

Every time he got the chance, Russell called Kemple collect at the apartment they had taken together in Fort Lauderdale. During the calls, Russell could sense Kemple's growing fear of being sick and alone, and this fueled Russell's determination to arrange an early departure from his current place of residence. But at the moment, a host of legal problems stood in his way.

In addition to the six months he owed the federal justice system for failing to report to prison on the fake passport conviction, the Harris County DA's office was pushing forward with a felony fraud charge it had filed against Russell in connection with his bogus slip-and-fall insurance claim. Now, back in custody, he faced the possibility of ten years in a Texas prison.

Amazingly, considering that he'd already jumped bail

once, pending his insurance fraud trial, Russell was being held on only a $45,000 bond. He could have been released by putting up ten percent of that amount—a mere $4500.

But for Russell, bail was never an option. Even if he'd made bail on the insurance fraud charge, Harris County officials would have immediately handed him over to the U.S. Marshals Service to begin serving his federal sentence. In Russell's mind, escape was his only choice. He knew, however, that it would instantly up the ante. So far, he was still pretty much a petty criminal. Sure, he'd jumped bail and eluded authorities for a year by working in the wholesale produce industry as a tomato buyer. But an escape would put him in an entirely different league. As a former police officer, he knew lawmen took escape seriously. If he stayed put and did his time, in a few years he could emerge from prison and possibly piece his life back together. If he tried to escape—whether he succeeded or not—life would never be the same.

It didn't take him long to make up his mind.

Harris County jailers assigned Russell to a dormitory-style pod on the ninth floor of the older jail. It was noisy and chaotic, and Russell looked for way to move to the sixth floor, with its quieter individual cells. Following his most recent suicide attempt, hospital doctors had inserted a heart catheter through Russell's groin, and the procedure had left his inner left thigh badly bruised. Before seeking medical attention for a legitimate concern, Russell intentionally aggravated the bruise. He squeezed, bashed and mashed the inside of his thigh with his hands until his groin looked like someone had kicked the hell out of him—which is exactly what he told the jail's medical staff had happened to him. After seeing the bruise, the doctors soon had Russell sent to the sixth floor, where he immediately began looking for an escape route.

That spring, Russell was sitting in the jail's dayroom watching the aftermath of the South Central riots in Los Angeles on television. During the newscast, an inmate Russell remembers only as Jessie, a small Hispanic man, walked by. Jessie was a trusty, an inmate who works a job in the jail and has more freedom to move about than other prisoners. Suddenly, Jessie stopped and turned around.

"Do you want a jailhouse job?" he asked Russell.

"Hell, yes!" replied Russell, jumping to his feet.

"Well, there's a job open in classification. All you gotta do is sit at a desk and write inmates' names on their classification folders as the deputies process them in."

"That job's got my name written on it with bright neon lights."

"Well, if you want it, you gotta pay. Pay a hundred dollars to my partner. One-time fee. But at least you get plenty of food and a chance to move."

Jessie explained that the $100 would have gone to him, but he was about to "catch the chain"—or be transferred from county jail to state prison. Since his partner—another trusty who worked as a typist—paid Jessie, Jessie figured it was only fair that Russell should pay his partner for the privilege of a jailhouse job.

"No problem," said Russell. Kemple was his banker, and the money would be in his jail account today. One of the jailers would be in touch with him, Jessie said, to collect the cash.

Two hours later the jailer appeared at his cell door. He was a white man in his early thirties, with a medium build, thinning brown hair, and a mustache.

"Pack your property," he said blandly. "You're moving to the seventh floor."

"All right!" Russell thought to himself as he followed the jailer down the hall. He knew that the seventh floor was where the trusties were housed. If nothing else, his living conditions were about to improve.

The next day Russell reported to work, helping deputies sort new inmates as they arrived. Three other inmate trusties worked in the classification office. The typist was a tall, muscular, 45-year-old Hispanic man covered with tattoos. Two other guys—one tall and skinny, the other short and fat—were assigned to line up inmates as they waited to be processed. All three had done time before and were well versed in the routines of jailhouse life.

In the booking drill, every inmate went through a five-step process that took from twelve to sixteen hours before ever reaching his cell. First, the prisoner was searched and questioned about his name, address, and other basic information. Then, he was fingerprinted and photographed. Next came a chat with a representative from the county's pretrial services office to see if the inmate qualified for a personal recognizance bond. After that was a medical screening, followed by a strip search, a shower, and the issuing of standard fluorescent orange jail attire. Finally, every new inmate passed through the classification office to be assigned to a cellblock that was supposedly compatible with his age, sex, sexuality, number of offenses, types of crimes, and both his security needs and the type of security threat he poses. For example, an 18-year-old arrested for the first time in his life for, say, auto theft, is not put in a cell with a pedophile serial killer. Additionally, homosexual prisoners who fear they will be vulnerable to abuse in the jail's general population can request to be placed on a floor segregated by sexuality. Theoretically, at least.

It was in this final stage of the process that Russell worked. Early on, he noticed that each inmate wore a wristband containing personal information and color-coded to designate where he was allowed to be at any given time. White was for general-population inmates at 1301 Franklin. Red-and-white stripes went to prisoners assigned to administrative segregation, better known as solitary confinement. Purple-and-white stripes were for general-population inmates at the newer jail at 701 San Jacinto. Homosexuals wore solid yellow bands. Inmate trusties allowed outside the jail wore orange wristbands, and inside trusties, like Russell, wore blue.

Initially, Russell considered stealing one of the orange bands worn by trusties with outside privileges. But there were three possible problems with that: timing, clothing, and the concern that someone might ask him what the hell he was doing. He decided against it. Eventually, he concluded that he would get hold of civilian clothes and somehow walk out the front door from the visitors' side of the jail. This would be the least dramatic way of escape, and would likely provide him with the longest possible lead time before any of the jailers noticed he was missing. If they don't know you're missing, they don't know to start looking for you.

As it happens, Harris County Jail has piles of civilian clothes on hand. When suspected criminals are arrested and brought in, they're wearing street clothes. After prisoners are booked, their clothes are stored in the basement of 1301 Franklin near where the intake process begins. Inconveniently for Russell, the classification office where he worked was on the second floor—close to the men's clothing storage area in the basement, but not close enough to reach it without being detected. Whenever he wasn't being watched, Russell went exploring. On one excursion, he ventured into the room on the northwest corner of the second floor where female inmates were processed. There he found a dumbwaiter used by female classification officers to send females' civilian clothes down to the basement. Better still, in front of the dumb-waiter he found a pile of women's clothing waiting to be sent down.

Russell quickly rummaged through the skirts, blouses, and slacks until he came across a pair of red stretch pants that would potentially fit him. He grabbed them and hurried to an area behind the male classification office where there were cells housing juvenile males about to be certified to stand trial as adults. Among the kids incarcerated there was a 16-year-old boy named Chris. At 5-foot-4 and 120 pounds or so, he was potentially vulnerable to inmate predators. Russell had become concerned for the kid's safety. Plus, in jail it never hurts to make a friend when you can. You never know when it might pay off.

"I really loved this kid, but not in a sexual way," Russell says. "He was very street smart. He never questioned anything I asked him to do. He felt like we were on a mission together."

Some time before, when Russell had offered a bit of protection, Chris gratefully accepted. So when Russell needed help, Chris didn't hesitate to return the favor.

"Here, hide these for me," said Russell, pushing the red pants through the cell bars and into Chris's hands. "I'll explain later."

Chris nodded.

Russell hurried back to the female classification office, again burrowed through the pile of clothes, and unearthed a large white T-shirt. He snatched it and headed back to the male classification office. There he grabbed a couple of teabags from a box next to the coffee pot, dashed back to Chris's cell, and handed him the shirt and tea bags.

"Tie dye this for me," Russell said.

Again, Chris agreed without questioning the strange request.

A day later, Russell had a brown stained T-shirt and a pair of red stretch pants. It was better than an orange jumpsuit. At best, Russell hoped he might pass himself off as an undercover cop, but he would need more props. On a recent visit to the infirmary, he had noticed a walkie-talkie in a charger inside the doctors' lounge. He decided he would steal it the night before he planned to make his break.

Swiping the walkie-talkie from the lounge and hiding it would not be easy. After much deliberation, Russell devised a solution based on his past work experience. As a young man in the produce business in Norfolk, Russell had earned the favor of corporate and government officials by plying them with lavish gift baskets of fresh fruits and vegetables. He figured a variation of that would work at the county jail.

Aside from the classification office, Russell's blue wristband also gave him access to the officers' dining hall. Every evening after the deputies finished eating, Russell started gathering the leftover sandwiches into a paper bag and taking them to the nurses in the jail infirmary where the coveted walkie-talkie was stored. Russell hoped to get on the good side of the head nurse, a stern type like Nurse Ratched in *One Flew Over the Cuckoo's Nest*. Inmates and guards alike referred to her as Five-by-Five: five feet tall, and five feet wide.

In addition to the walkie-talkie, Russell would need unfettered access to a less secure area of the jail. Over the next few weeks, he continued to study jail security— when the inmate population was counted, when the guards took their breaks. Kemple flew into Houston to visit him a couple of times. On each occasion, Russell grilled him thoroughly about the lobby's layout, front desk procedures, and anything else he could think of.

On May 12, 1992, Russell put his plan in motion. First stop, the officers' dining hall on the tenth floor, where he stuffed leftovers into a paper bag. Next, the infirmary. After diverting Nurse Five-by-Five's attention with a hamburger, Russell grabbed the sick bay walkie-talkie and stashed it in the sandwich bag. Hurrying around the corner, he hid the bag between the hallway wall and some exposed pipes near the administrative segregation cells, where Chris was housed and Russell's escape outfit was hidden.

The following evening, Friday the 13th, Russell called A. D. Ghinaudo, a former co-worker, to see if he was home. Russell had been Ghinaudo's boss at White Swan, the food distribution company in Houston. Under Russell, Ghinaudo had been White Swan's number one salesman, and the two men had had a good working relationship. When Ghinaudo answered, Russell hung up. That was all he needed to know. He then made his way over to the juvie lock-up to see Chris.

"Hey, kid," said Russell to the young inmate. "I made early parole, and I need those things I gave you. You got 'em?"

"Yeah, I got 'em."

Glancing up and down the hall, he raised his mattress, grabbed the pants and T-shirt, and shoved them through the bars into Russell's eager hands.

"Take me with you," Chris whispered.

"Can't do it, but thanks for your help," Russell whispered back.

He headed toward the male classification office. Right on schedule, the guards were taking their cigarette break. Russell quickly slipped out of his jumpsuit, donned the T-shirt and pants, put the jumpsuit back on over them, and stuck his head inside the office door.

"I'm going back upstairs to my cell to take a dump," he told his three co-workers.

Carrying the walkie-talkie in the bag, he caught the elevator and took it to the 13th floor, the location of the jail's gymnasium, which is closed at night. He stripped off the jumpsuit and threw it and the paper bag out of the elevator and into the dark and empty gym. Now dressed in T-shirt and red pants, holding the walkie-talkie in one hand, he rode the elevator back down to the 10th floor. When the elevator doors slid open, Russell stepped out. Two deputies stood in the hallway. Another sat inside a glass-enclosed booth, behind the electronic panel that controlled the two sliding metal doors that stood between Russell and the visitors' area. None of the officers recognized him. Russell had only been an inmate for about a month, and he was just one of almost 5,000 inmates crammed into six floors of the 13-story building.

As nonchalantly as he could, his heart practically popping out of his chest, Russell walked past the two deputies, then tapped on the control-booth window with the walkie-talkie, taking care to avoid eye contact with any of the guards. So loudly that it startled him, the thick steel doors began sliding apart. Making sure not to move too quickly, Russell stepped through the opening. He was now on the visitors' side, but he wasn't yet free.

Still striving to keep his composure, Russell slowly walked across the visitors' area to another set of elevators and punched the down button. Seconds passed like hours until the elevator arrived. It was empty. He stepped inside and hit the button. It didn't stop until the first floor.

As he stepped out of the elevator, he expected to be in the jail's lobby. Instead, he was stunned to see that a pair of solid glass doors still separated him from the lobby and the jail's public entrance. He walked up to the doors and pushed. To his horror, they didn't open.

His mind was spinning now, he was dizzy, and he feared he might pass out from the overload of adrenaline surging through his bloodstream. Somehow regaining his composure, he noticed that if he simply pushed on the metal bar across the middle of the door, the door would open. He opened the door and walked into the lobby. There was no going back now.

As he made his way to the front doors, he partially covered his face by pretending to speak into the walkie-talkie. At any moment, he expected to be grabbed, tackled, or shot. But nothing happened. He kept on walking. No one shouted for him to stop. No one slapped a pair of handcuffs around his wrists. No one put him in a headlock or wrestled him to the ground. No bullets flew past his head.

And then he was outside.

Russell turned to his left, walked about ten yards across a courtyard, and then down the steep, wide cement stairs that lead to Franklin Street, one of downtown Houston's northernmost thoroughfares. As he walked along Franklin, the first car he spotted coming towards him was a silver four-door Mercedes-Benz with a *Ross Perot for President* sticker on its front bumper. Odds were that the owner was a God-fearing, America-loving, law-abiding patriot more than willing to do a favor for a lawman in need. So Russell decided to bet the farm. He'd been a police officer, and he knew how to get a driver to stop his car. Waving his borrowed walkie-talkie, Russell stepped in front of the oncoming vehicle and motioned for the driver to halt, and then to roll down his window.

"Excuse me, sir," Russell said. "I'm Officer Stevens, and I really need to get to the Hyatt Regency. Could you please give me a lift over there? It sure would be a big help."

"Well, sure," the driver replied. "Get in."

"I'm supposed to meet my wife over there," Russell said as he climbed in. "She'll bring me back to the parking lot and jump-start my car. I really appreciate this. You know how women can be."

"I sure do," the driver said.

"So, do you think Perot can win?" Russell asked.

"Not sure. But he's better than Bush."

"He's got my vote," Russell said. "I can't stand the Bush family."

"Everybody's tired of career politicians," the driver concurred.

As the Mercedes wound through the nighttime streets of Houston, the driver seemed not to notice how absurd Russell looked in his red stretch pants. Russell made sure to keep the police radio displayed prominently in his lap.

"I can't believe that car of mine wouldn't start," said Russell as they approached the Hyatt. "I screwed up and left the parking lights on when I went on duty."

"That'll do it," the man said. "Well, here we are. Where do you want to get out?"

"Just pull up in the unloading zone. She's supposed to be in the lobby waiting on me."

"Okay," said the driver, slowing the Mercedes to a stop. "Good luck."

Conveniently for Russell, the Mercedes owner had not been an especially talkative or inquisitive soul, and Russell had had time to listen to the chatter on his stolen police radio as they drove to the hotel. So far, the jail guards hadn't missed him.

On any given night, the Houston Hyatt Regency is a fairly bustling place. Out front, taxis line up eight to ten deep waiting for fares. Inside the lobby are the registration desk, bellhops, a couple of restaurants, a sunken bar and, naturally, security personnel—both uniformed and plainclothed. Russell opted to use the hotel's rear entrance.

Inside the Hyatt, Russell headed for the pay phones and made another call to his former White Swan coworker Ghinaudo. His luck was holding. Ghinaudo was still home and answered the phone himself. Russell told him that he was at the Hyatt, that he had just been robbed of his money and belongings. He asked Ghinaudo to bring him some clothes and $300 so he could get back home to Virginia.

Ghinaudo agreed and didn't ask any questions. He did not know what Russell was up to, or even that Russell had been in jail. Before leaving his house, Ghinaudo told his wife what he was doing.

"I know it sounds strange," Ghinaudo told her. "But this man has always been good to me. I owe him. And now he needs my help."

Which is exactly the way Russell had hoped he would react.

As he waited for Ghinaudo to arrive, Russell phoned James Kemple. He'd made bond, he told him, and he'd be back home in Miami the next morning. Next he entered a stall of the men's room and shed his red stretch pants. Now wearing only his shirt and two pairs of boxer shorts—a light blue pair over a white pair—Russell found a private spot on a couch near the phones and waited for Ghinaudo, making sure to keep his legs crossed. It wasn't an ideal situation. But, in case the police were already looking for a man in red stretch pants, he had to ditch them. He also kept an ear to the police radio for any transmissions about his escape.

About 50 minutes later, Ghinaudo finally arrived at the Hyatt. Russell changed into the borrowed clothes—a pair of gray polyester slacks that were big in the waist and too short, a blue plaid shirt, and a Houston Astros cap. He then asked his friend to drive him north toward Houston Intercontinental Airport, the larger of the city's two airports, now known as Bush Intercontinental, and leave him at the last motel before the rental car drop-offs.

Russell thanked Ghinaudo for his help, checked into the budget motel and headed for his room. Just as he closed the door, he heard the first reference to himself on the police radio.

"All units, be on the lookout for a Steven J. Russell who escaped from the Harris County Jail this evening," said the dispatcher through a crackle of radio static. "Suspect is a white male, last seen wearing red pants and T-shirt."

Russell, a former cop with a knowledge of police radio jargon, picked up the walkie-talkie.

"Patrol to base," he said into the radio. "This is unit 351. Over."

"Base to patrol," the dispatcher replied. "Go ahead 351."

"Roger that. Responding to your BOL [be on the lookout] on Steven Russell. I'm not positive, but I believe I may have seen someone matching the description of your suspect on Broadway near Hobby Airport."

In mock-sadness, Russell explained to the dispatcher that unit 351 was now in the western part of Harris County, miles and miles from Hobby, the city's older, smaller airport in south Houston. Obviously, he added, he was too far away to help with the search. But he wished them good luck.

After signing off, Russell got on the telephone and set up another diversion. Using his own name, he booked a flight to Norfolk leaving from Hobby at eleven o'clock the next morning. It was a flight he had no intention of taking. By now, it was close to midnight, too late to catch a flight from Intercontinental. Using an alias (which he still refuses to reveal), he reserved a seat on a Saturday morning flight to Miami. He then called Kemple and told him to meet him at the Miami airport the next morning.

To make sure Jimmy wasn't under surveillance by police, Russell told him he would be on the morning's second flight from Houston. In truth, Russell was booked on the first one, paying for it with the money Ghinaudo had loaned him.

After landing in Miami, Russell headed straight to a pay phone and called the Miami-Dade Police Department's dispatch office.

"Metro dispatch," answered the dispatcher.

"Hello, this is Trooper Stevens with the Florida Highway Patrol," Russell said. "I'm at the airport and thought I heard something about a BOL. Are y'all looking for someone out here?"

The dispatcher double-checked with his co-workers, and then informed Russell that there was no BOL currently in effect at that airport. Russell was still in the clear. Out in the terminal area, when he finally spotted Jimmy, he quietly walked up behind him and grabbed him by the arm.

"Let's get out of here," Russell said. "I've got some things to tell you."

Russell couldn't yet confess to Kemple the real circumstances of his sudden departure from Harris County Jail. But he didn't need to. Not long after the two men arrived back at Kemple's Miami Beach apartment, Jimmy's mother was on the phone informing her son that his boyfriend was a fugitive.

Russell wasn't exactly sure how Mrs. Kemple had learned that he was on the run, but guessed she might have found out from the police. He worried that the authorities might have Jimmy's new address, so he and Kemple headed for the Marriott, where they spent the weekend making plans to fly out of the country. On Monday, Kemple left the hotel, drove to his bank, and withdrew enough money for Russell to catch a flight to Mexico. They planned for Russell to leave the country first. Kemple would join him a week later in Mexico City.

It might have worked, if not for two glitches. First, Russell got sentimental. Second, he and Kemple made the mistake of telling Kemple's mom they were leaving the country. Apparently, Helen Kemple didn't think running off to Mexico with a fugitive was in her ailing son's best interests. That same Monday, Russell rented a car and drove to the Miami airport. Just as he was set to board his flight, he changed his mind. He didn't want to leave without Kemple. So he left the terminal and started back to the parking lot. But before he reached his car, two U.S. Marshals grabbed him and took him to the Dade County Jail.

"They knew exactly what I was driving and where I was going," Russell says. "I was pissed."

The next day in Miami, Russell appeared before a magistrate for arraignment. For the sake of expediency, and figuring he could do as good a job as a public defender, Russell decided to represent himself. He argued that since his home was nearby in West Palm Beach, he should be freed on bond pending his next court appearance. Amazingly, Judge Murray Myerson set Russell's bond at $20,000. Russell never forgot the judge's kindness.

"Two years later, I voted for him using Jim's name," he says.

chapter nine

Love on the Run

After bonding out of the Dade County Jail, Russell resumed his plan to leave the country. He got the bondsman to drive him back to Jimmy's house, and he and Jimmy then drove back to the airport, where they caught separate planes to Mexico City. Russell was now committed to what would become a decade-long game of cat-and-mouse with state and federal authorities.

On the flight down, he passed part of the time by writing a letter to U.S. District Judge David Hittner, who had given him the six-month sentence for passport fraud. In the letter, he apologized to the judge for not turning himself in. But in fact, he was trying to throw the authorities off his trail. Instead of mailing it from Mexico, Russell gave the note to a flight attendant bound for the Dominican Republic, who mailed it from Santo Domingo.

After arriving in Mexico City, Russell says he also placed a phone call to Harris County Sheriff Johnny Klevenhagen (who is now deceased).

"Sheriff, this is Steven Russell," he said. "I just wanted to let you know that I'm sorry I had to leave. But I'm down here in the Dominican Republic. Oh, and one other thing. I hope you don't blame my escape on those guards who were outside taking a smoke break. Actually, you could fix the problem if you allowed smoking back in the jail."

"Fuck you," replied Klevenhagen, a man known to sometimes have quite a temper.

Russell hung up. From now on, he would be a fugitive.

In Mexico City, with the help of an investment-banker friend in Florida, Russell soon landed some consulting work for a small oil company.

"I get jobs easily," he says, "because I am capable of selling myself."

Russell hoped he could move the company into the food service business, and perhaps make it the food-distribution king of Mexico. Even as a wanted man, Russell felt a need to stay busy. He had started as a child on the loading docks of his family's produce warehouse in Norfolk. By the time he graduated from high school, he was already managing some important aspects of the business.

"I love to work," Russell says. "No one will ever accuse me of being lazy. And I strive for perfection."

But Russell could not sell the Mexican company on his idea of moving into food distribution and, soon, he grew bored with Mexico City.

"I really didn't want to live there," he says. "I was also concerned that Jim would not receive adequate health care there."

So they returned to the United States, flying first to New York City, then moving on to Philadelphia, staying in each city about a month. For the most part, they lived quietly and avoided drawing attention to themselves. Russell worked grunt jobs at restaurants to avoid dipping into the money he says he placed in Kemple's bank account and various other accounts—about which he prefers not to elaborate, giving the impression that some of it may still be out there.

Even though they were on the run, Russell insists, his relationship with Kemple flourished. But Kemple, his health failing, grew homesick for Florida. In July, after Russell lined up a job running a fast food restaurant in Miami, they headed south—close to the very spot where Russell had last escaped from custody.

"By that time, I figured the search for us would have cooled off," he says. "Plus, Miami is a lot different than Palm Beach. Palm Beach is cliquish. But in Miami, you can blend into the crowd. It's a world of its own. I love it there. Beautiful people everywhere."

In Miami Beach, Russell and Kemple leased a one-bedroom place at the Flamingo Plaza Apartments, a little art-deco place that now glowed at night with neon lights just three blocks away from a police station. It was also near the ocean, and Russell and Kemple spent most of their time sunning on the beach, or swimming, or watching television at home. They carefully steered clear of gay bars, fearing police might be searching the clubs for them. They rode out Hurricane Andrew barricaded inside their apartment.

"It sounded like a runaway freight train," Russell remembers. "I tried to sleep through it, but Jimmy kept waking me up with updates every half-hour or so. He was like a kid in a candy store. He listened to the news on a little portable Walkman. Then he got horny, and we had sex through the later stages of the storm. How many chances do you get to make love when the wind is blowing 155 miles per hour? I wasn't going to argue."

Russell loved to work, but the longer he stayed at the fast food restaurant, the more he hated it. It was a three-outlet fast-food chain and its decor evoked every cliché about Florida, down to the hot pink flamingos painted on the walls. He'd gotten the job by responding to an ad in the *Miami Herald*. Using a bogus name, he had portrayed himself as the founder of a San Francisco produce company who had sold his business and wanted a job just to stay busy. He was hired without a background check. Russell started out managing the branch of the restaurant on Hallendale Beach Boulevard. He and the two other managers worked ten hours a day, six days a week.

In October, not long after starting, Russell was transferred to the chain's newest outlet on Biscayne Boulevard in North Miami Beach. There, the job got tougher.

"My back and physical work don't mix," says Russell, referring to the near-fatal automobile accident in Houston in 1986 which still caused him pain when he stood for long periods, or sat in a chair without a back.

"My boss turned out to be a real asshole," he continues. "When I was working to get the new store ready to open, I brought in a chair with a back on it for the manager's office. When boss saw it, he threw it in the garbage can, and he humiliated the hell out of me in front of the other employees. Right then and there, I decided he would pay for that mistake."

While preparing the restaurant for its grand opening, Russell pocketed one of the three programmer keys to the new computerized cash register. When the restaurant opened and money was flowing in, Russell began rewarding himself with a daily cash bonus for his efforts.

"I began to steal proceeds from the cash register by screwing up the program on the register's computer," he says. "I would rework the entire day's sales by resetting the clock on the cash register and clearing out the running totals. That way, they could never tell that the money collected didn't equal the money taken in. Plus, I worked from 6:00 P.M. until the 2:00 A.M. closing. While the other employees cleaned the restaurant, I cleaned out the register."

Each day that he worked there, from October to Thanksgiving weekend, Russell walked off with about an extra $250 in cash. Management never noticed the missing money until after Russell had left, when revenue at the new restaurant suddenly spiked dramatically. The company contacted the police, and a North Miami Beach detective came to question Russell at his apartment. Russell told the detective that he didn't know what he was talking about, and advised him that he had better drop the matter before Russell filed a lawsuit against both the cop and the company. Russell must have been persuasive, since the investigation was quickly dropped. Nevertheless, Russell and Jimmy began packing for a colder climate.

While working at the restaurant, Russell had come across an ad in the *Wall Street Journal* for a job with

NutraSweet as the company's director of North American sales. About two months after sending his résumé, using Kemple's name, to the Chicago-based company, Russell got a call. After flying up for an interview, he was offered the position at $85,000 a year. This time, Russell says, he was hired on his own merits, not because of an enhanced résumé. Overlooking Kemple's name at the top, this résumé was mostly true—with the exception of a statement that he'd owned a produce company in San Francisco that he'd recently sold to a group of Mexican investors. Russell landed the job, beating out 650 other applicants—many of whom were probably more qualified, at least on paper.

"I can read a balance sheet as well as any CPA," contends Russell.

But it was his ability to analyze people quickly and figure out what they need, he says, that actually got him the job.

"I'm persuasive because I understand and listen to people. I study everything about a person. No detail is too small. People love to talk, and I love to listen. Listening to a person is the key to being able to outwit them."

In January 1993, Russell and Kemple moved to Chicago. At first they rented a $1,700-a-month, two-bedroom apartment in a high-rise on the edge of downtown. Kemple loved it there because he could walk almost everywhere he needed to go. But soon they bought a house in suburban Grayslake, a two-story with four bedrooms and three baths, for $200,000.

They did not socialize in Chicago. Instead, they took turns cooking each other gourmet meals at home. They also stayed on the road a good deal. Russell's work at NutraSweet included a lot of day trips, and he often took Kemple with him. All the while, Kemple's health was getting worse, but Russell was determined that his companion's quality of life would change as little as possible. Russell cooked and cleaned, he bought Kemple's medicines and made sure he took them every day. Since Russell worked at NutraSweet under Kemple's name, Kemple would have health insurance to cover his mounting medical expenses for as long as Russell worked there.

"I knew he was dying," Russell says. "I wanted to spend as much time as I could with him, and make his life as fun and as comfortable as possible."

Russell hoped the trips away from Chicago would prevent lawmen from zeroing in on their location. The outings also provided both of them opportunities to phone family members without the authorities, whom Russell feared might be listening, tracing the calls back to the fugitives' well-appointed hideout.

"I'm certain the feds were totally fucking confused with calls coming in [to his and Kemple's relatives] from all over the fucking country," Russell says proudly. "They must have thought I was out robbing banks."

In addition to the health insurance coverage he had fraudulently signed up for as James Kemple, Russell also, through NutraSweet's providers, took out several life insurance policies in Kemple's name. He also padded his expense account. During ten months with the company, Russell claimed $45,000 in bogus business expenses.

In November 1993, NutraSweet officials uncovered Russell's phony expense reporting during a routine audit. He was only discovered, he says, because he was being a conscientious employee.

"I was too busy selling NutraSweet, and not busy enough doing my expense reports," he says. "I waited until the end of the month to file my expense reports, and that was a big mistake in a big organization."

Russell could have faced significant criminal charges. But he discovered that corporations would often prefer to fire a dishonest employee rather than file charges that could generate bad publicity. So, NutraSweet terminated Russell, but brought no charges against him. It was a scenario he would remember.

Before he and Kemple left Chicago, Russell converted his CIGNA group insurance policy to an individual plan. The life insurance policy in Kemple's name was worth

$500,000. Seven months later, in May 1994, Russell sold that policy to a viatical company. A viatical is a perfectly legal company that buys life insurance policies from terminally ill people for a fraction of the policy's value. The person selling the policy gets the benefit of at least some money while he is still alive and can enjoy it, and the purchaser receives the full value of the policy when the former policyholder dies.

He then sold the $500,000 life insurance policy for $330,000. According to Russell, Kemple spent $10,000 of the money on a ring for his mother. He and Kemple also used $40,000 for a down payment on a house they were having built in Coral Springs, Florida. They stashed the rest of the money in various bank accounts.

All the while, Kemple's health had deteriorated to the point that he could no longer do many basic things for himself. Russell, who had rarely changed his own daughter's dirty diapers when she was an infant, now cleaned and bathed Jimmy daily. When Kemple could no longer digest food and stopped eating, Russell spent $1,000 a week on TPN—Total Parenteral Nutrition, a substance that intravenously feeds people who can't take nourishment orally.

Knowing he didn't have long to live, Kemple wanted to return to Florida to be near his mother, so Russell again sent out résumés under Kemple's name. In January 1994, he landed a job in West Palm Beach as vice-president of finance for Diversified Communications Industries, Ltd. Among other things, DCI subcontracted with Bell South to lay fiber optic cable in Florida and South Carolina. DCI also had a subsidiary by the name of Plastaview, which manufactured postcard display racks. Together, the two companies had annual revenues of $18 million.

Russell's contract called for him to receive $75,000 a year to oversee the finance departments of both DCI and Plastaview. But after a few days on the job, he made the unilateral decision that each company should pay him that amount.

"Basically, since I was writing the checks, I collected two paychecks instead of one—one from each company," he says. "So I was actually making $150,000."

The gravy train lasted about four months, until Russell's internal alarm—some sort of con man's sixth sense—told him that DCI officials were about to catch on to him. He abruptly resigned in April 1994. Russell and Kemple then went back underground, renting from a landlord who required no background check.

"I had the phone listed in an alias name, along with the power and the water," says Russell. "We told Jim's mom to never call us there from her home. We were non-existent."

Before leaving DCI, though, just as he had done at NutraSweet, Russell again obtained health and life insurance through the company in Kemple's name. This time he purchased several policies: one from CNA Insurance for $200,000 worth of coverage; a Banker Life Assurance policy worth $50,000; a CIGNA policy for $150,000; and one from Providence Life for $100,000.

As Russell had anticipated, shortly after his sudden departure DCI officials became suspicious, and soon discovered the extra paychecks Russell had been issuing himself. This time, DCI asked the West Palm Beach police department to investigate the man they had known as James Kemple. One of the investigators' first stops was the home of Helen Kemple, James's mother.

"One of the detectives noticed all the numbers for insurance companies I had in my Rolodex at DCI," Russell says. "Then some of Helen's neighbors told the police that Jimmy had AIDS, so they started putting the picture together."

Russell and Jimmy had kept in contact with Helen, even though they suspected that Helen had reported Russell's whereabouts to the Florida authorities after his first escape in 1992. After that incident, Russell says Kemple raised hell with his mother and that she was loyal to both of them from that point forward. Indeed, this time, according to Russell, Helen Kemple obeyed her son's wishes and didn't give Russell up.

West Palm Beach police detective Mike Scoggin tried to speak to Helen.

"[Russell's] lover's mother was obviously in cahoots with him, without question," says Scoggin. "When I knocked on [her] door, she would not come out, and just peeked through, and wouldn't say anything."

But, says the officer, Helen was not the only person in the Fort Lauderdale area cooperating with Russell—some willingly, some not.

"[Russell] had everybody duped," continues Scoggin. "He was going to [exclusive clubs] here all the time. He had all these rich socialite friends. He ran in the right circles. He is the modern day con man. He's good. There's no question about it."

Scoggin contacted the Florida Department of Motor Vehicles and asked for copies of Kemple's driver's license photographs. Russell, trying to stay one step ahead of his pursuer, also contacted the driver's license office and found out that Scoggin had requested Kemple's photos. Later, Russell called again, this time impersonating Scoggin, and canceled the detective's request. Scoggin says he doubts Russell's version of the chase. Russell says don't be so sure.

"Remember, I used to be a cop," Russell explains. "There wasn't a book or manual I didn't read on the use of information retrieval."

The move bought Russell time, but not much. Despite the cancellation, Scoggin soon obtained the pictures of Kemple, and he arranged to have a local newspaper publish them.

The photos appeared on June 10, 1994—the same day Russell started a new $55,000-a-year job with Eli Witt as director of sales for the company's Miami distribution center. It was a job much like Russell's old produce-industry jobs, only Witt specialized in supplying convenience stores with tobacco and candy. Russell had only been on the job about an hour when he received a call from Kemple. Jimmy's doctor had called to say that the morning paper was carrying Jimmy's name and his picture, along with a story about how police were looking for him and Russell. Since Russell had used Kemple's name to get the job at Witt, he quietly slipped out of the office and never returned.

Meanwhile, phone calls poured into the police department. Luckily for Russell, it was Scoggin's day off, a break that allowed him and Kemple enough time to flee. Using false names and paying in cash, they purchased one-way first class seats on a U.S. Airways flight from Fort Lauderdale to Philadelphia. In Philadelphia, they checked into the Ritz-Carlton Hotel on Rittenhouse Square.

The next morning around 9:00 A.M.—by odd happenstance, the same day O. J. Simpson was arrested—the two went to Meridian Bank to begin withdrawing funds from some of their accounts. Then Russell made a huge mistake: He agreed to let Jimmy handle the transaction. Jimmy didn't even want Russell to be there. He was desperate to show Russell, and probably himself, that he could still manage his affairs. Russell gave him the chance.

Simply put, Kemple was not nearly as skillful a liar as Russell. Whatever he said, it obviously concerned bank officials. Kemple later told Russell that the bank manager had immediately seemed suspicious and began dragging her feet, perhaps suspecting Kemple was being forced to withdraw the money against his will. Under questioning from the bank manager, Kemple went to pieces.

Back at the Ritz-Carlton, where Russell was ordering a leisurely room-service breakfast of steak and eggs, his internal alarm failed him. When Kemple had still not returned an hour later, Russell telephoned the bank. Bank officials would not allow Kemple to speak to Russell for long, but Kemple did manage to utter a predetermined code word that let Russell know things weren't going well. Soon a lieutenant from the Philadelphia police department came on the line and ordered Russell to come to the bank. Russell told him to fuck off.

Despite his bravado, Russell was now scared for himself, but even more so for Kemple. He tried to call Helen but couldn't reach her. He tried to call an attorney he knew in Philadelphia. No luck. Then he made another mistake. Although he was sitting in a hotel room with $35,000 he and Kemple had withdrawn from First Union Bank in Florida the day before, he decided to take the time to finish breakfast before making his next move. While he dawdled, the police were able to coerce Kemple into telling them where he and Russell were staying. Before Russell had finished his meal, ten police officers were gathered outside his room. After more than two years as a fugitive, there was nowhere for him to run.

The Philadelphia police took Russell to the federal building downtown and placed him in one of the U.S. Marshals Service's holding tanks. Russell couldn't see Kemple, but he could hear him crying in an adjacent cell. It was the first time Kemple had been in trouble, much less incarcerated, and he was not handling it well. Between the bank fraud and passport fraud charges, Russell faced the possibility of five years or longer in federal prison. In Kemple's mind, it was all his fault. Between sobs, he begged Russell to forgive him.

"Of course I forgive you, silly boy," Russell said. He felt guilty for dragging Kemple into this mess. "Don't worry about me. I'll be okay. What we need to do is to get you out of here. You're too sick to be in jail. Hell, I would have told you to tell them."

Russell and Kemple were both charged with federal bank fraud for the DCI insurance scam. That night, Kemple was released on bond to his mother in Florida. Russell was sent to his new home: the federal correctional facility in Fairton, New Jersey.

Before his extradition back to Texas, during his six months at the federal correctional facility in New Jersey, Russell occasionally received mail from both his adoptive brother and mother. One message from his mother was especially interesting. For his birthday in September 1994, Georgia Russell sent her adopted son a $25 money order and a short, odd note.

"I'm so happy you are being taken care of," she wrote, giving credence to some statements made by Russell family friends, such as Reverend Sentell, that, by that time, Georgia Russell had become frightened of her adopted son.

In addition to his mother, as well as his brother Scott, Russell also corresponded with Kemple from prison. For a couple of weeks, Russell received letters from Jimmy almost every day. They were "the kindest letters anyone could ever write their lover," recalls Russell. He also called Kemple from the prison every day around noon. Two days before their final conversation, Jimmy's doctor estimated that he had about three months to live. Jimmy told Russell he was ready to die, that he was at peace with his fate. But the next day, he seemed to be struggling to remain upbeat.

"I've hit rock bottom," he sighed into the telephone.

"What do you mean?" asked Russell.

"I have to wear a diaper now," Kemple replied in a defeated tone. "I can't keep from shitting myself. The Sandostatin isn't working anymore."

"Well, nobody knows that except me and your mom and your sister, and we're not going to tell anybody. Hell, it's just part of life. I told you I had to wear diapers for a while after my car wreck."

But there was no consoling Kemple. If he could just gain a little weight back, he said, then he could function a little better and do some things for himself instead of having his sister and mother waiting on him constantly. He was afraid he would die before Russell was released. If he could just live until he was thirty...

Don't worry, Russell told him, federal prison was like a country club. He also said he was working on getting permission to have a U.S. marshal escort him to Florida to visit Jimmy.

Kemple was tiring now, so he thanked Russell for taking care of him. Except for a final "I love you," it was always the last thing Kemple said before hanging up. Russell figured it was because Kemple always felt like each of their conversations might be the last. This time he was right. On July 17, 1994, a little more than a month after their arrest in Philadelphia, Kemple died at his mother's house in Royal Palm Beach, Florida. He was 28. His mother, sister, and three dogs were with him.

The following day when Russell made his usual midday call, he received the news of Kemple's death. He was devastated.

"I can't tell you how much we loved each other," he says, still hurting eight years later.

As awful as it was, James Kemple's illness inspired one of Steven Russell's most successful legal maneuvers. It was a tactic that dovetailed perfectly with Russell's introduction to one of his fellow inmates: Dr. Richard Kones, a man Russell calls his special angel.

Shortly after his arrival at Fairton, Russell learned that Kemple's doctor had agreed to write a letter to federal prosecutors informing them that Kemple would soon die from AIDS. When the assistant U.S. attorney in charge of the case agreed to have the charges against Kemple dismissed, Russell immediately saw a possible way out of his own federal legal problems.

The fact that Russell was not HIV-positive nor, at 250 pounds, did he look like a dying man did not deter him. With coaching from Dr. Kones, a small gray-haired man, Russell soon began exhibiting symptoms associated with

HIV and AIDS. He stopped eating, lost weight, and became incontinent.

"The good doctor taught me everything he knew about HIV," Russell says. "He left out no detail, and I made a shitload of notes of our discussions. Look at any clinical book on the subject, and that's what I learned from the doctor."

(Unlike most other episodes of his life, Russell avoids going into much detail about his time with Kones or why the doctor agreed to help him. Kones, who at the time of this writing remains in the federal prison system, did not respond to written requests for an interview.)

Using the federal prison's typewriters, Russell altered his lab reports to indicate that he was in the final stages of AIDS. He then forwarded those reports to the prison medical staff by mail. "By November," he says, laughing, "I was looking horrible on paper."

Next, federal prosecutors received a letter written on the doctor's stationery—which Kones managed to keep in his cell—explaining that Russell had been diagnosed with AIDS in 1990.

"It is with great sadness I tell you, Mr. Russell is in the final stages of his illness and will soon succumb to it within the next months," the letter said.

Because of the work of Detective Scoggin of the West Palm Beach police, federal authorities believed that all the money from Russell's DCI insurance scam had been recovered. That misconception, combined with Russell's apparent declining health, convinced prosecutors with the U.S. Attorney's office in Philadelphia to drop the federal charges against him.

This did not end his legal problems. In December 1994, Russell was extradited to Texas to face the felony insurance fraud and escape charges that awaited him in Harris County.

"I think Texas would have extradited me even if I had been in fucking Europe," says Russell.

Texas, especially the Harris County sheriff's office, had not forgotten about Steven Russell. They wanted him back, HIV-positive or not. But as the saying goes, you have to be careful what you wish for.

chapter ten

The Big Con

Ex-convicts fresh out of prison often find themselves bouncing from menial job to menial job. For Steven Russell, that simply would not do. So, upon his parole from the Texas prison system in October 1995, after serving nine months of his three-year sentence for insurance fraud, Russell decided to improve his odds. He bought some new suits, had a little touch-up plastic surgery done around his eyes, and began intensely seeking a high-paying job, preferably one that would provide access to even more money.

First, Russell placed ads in the *Houston Chronicle* for nonexistent jobs with a make-believe Fortune 500 Company. The response was fantastic.

"I put an ad in the paper for an accounting manager, a controller, and a chief financial officer," he says. "And I used my address as the respondent for the ad. Once the résumés came in, I picked the best ones, and put my own résumé together from them."

The responses to his ads also let Russell know what kind of competition he would face in the job market. So on his new and improved résumé, he laid claim to a law degree from the University of Tennessee. He described himself as "a team player relating well to people at all levels." He claimed to have served as chief financial officer of a $150 million division of Prudential, said that he had developed software in conjunction with IBM, and that in both 1982 and 1990 he had been named employee of the year. Then, before sending out any bogus résumés, he set up accounts with two telephone answering services—one in Memphis and one in Fort Lauderdale, Florida.

"When the answering service answered the phone, they answered it as Prudential Insurance at both locations," he explains. "When someone left a message, I returned the call, and gave myself a favorable recommendation."

In preparation for the interviews he anticipated, Russell spent hours at a time at the Houston Public Library, where he researched health maintenance organizations and managed care.

"I also contacted people who were in the HMO business, and tried to learn as much as I could about the business so that I could carry myself in an interview," he says.

Armed with his fantasy résumé, Russell scanned the *Houston Chronicle* classifieds for jobs that could finance the lifestyle he envisioned for himself and Phillip Morris. In early January 1996, he spotted a notice for an $85,000-a-year insurance industry position listed by Baldwin & Associates, a headhunting company. Russell sent in his bogus list of qualifications and activated his answering service accounts. A few days later, a Baldwin representative called, and arranged for Russell to speak with the company's president, Gary Baldwin. During their telephone discussion, Russell determined that Baldwin's client was in the managed health care business, North American Medical Management. He was invited to come in for an interview. To accelerate his research, Russell contacted an insurance company named NYL Care, and posed as a state senate legislative aide who was writing a position paper on HMOs for his boss. An NYL Care official amazingly invited Russell to come by the company's Houston office, Russell says, where he picked up some useful buzzwords.

"For example, 'bed days per 1,000' and 'capitalization' are a couple of the terms they use while discussing revenue," he says.

Russell was an adept student, and his research paid off.

After he aced his initial interview with the company, North American Medical Management, or NAMM, he was flown to Nashville for a second grilling by the company's top executives. The next day, one of the NAMM executives made calls to verify Russell's references.

"[He] thought he was calling Prudential," Russell says, "but it was the answering service I had set up. [He] called, and I returned the call the next day, disguising my voice."

On January 23, 1996—less than four months after he had been granted parole—Russell became the chief financial officer of North American Medical Management.

Don Holmquist is no fool, and he has the credentials to prove it. Unlike Steven Russell, Holmquist actually holds a law degree. More impressively, although he never flew on a mission, Holmquist is also a former member of NASA's stable of space shuttle astronauts. After leaving NASA, Holmquist amassed a small fortune by launching, or helping to launch, several small business ventures, including North American Medical Management, Inc., a company designed to coordinate the financial affairs of independent practice associations that represent doctors and groups of doctors in Houston.

The late 1980s and early 1990s saw the advent of managed health care, and the health maintenance organizations (HMOs) that followed. When HMOs placed caps on how much money they would pay their affiliated physicians per year, doctors found themselves in need of companies to oversee the business side of their practices while they cared for patients. In 1991, Holmquist teamed up with investors Herb Fitch and Jeff Rothenberger to create just such a company. Although its parent company, PhyCor, was based in Nashville, Tennessee, NAMM operated out of a high-rise office building on the North Loop in Holmquist's adopted hometown of Houston, where he had lived during his years with the space program.

Holmquist and his partners convinced nineteen independent physicians' associations, representing almost 2,000 individual doctors, to sign on with NAMM. Business was brisk, which placed considerable pressure on the company's chief financial officer, the person charged with keeping watch over of all the clients and their standing with insurance companies. NAMM's original CFO quit after just a couple of years on the job, and he had been succeeded by a host of short-lived replacements. None of them, it seems, was quite up to the job.

In January 1996, NAMM officials thought they finally had the problem solved when they hired an outgoing 39-year-old man with a quick smile and gregarious nature who seemed conscientious and hardworking.

"Steven Russell is a likable guy," Holmquist admits. "And he was easier to work with than your average chief financial officer. Your average CFO is not the most exciting person to talk to. They tend to be a little bit devoted to details. But Steve Russell was engaging. Aside from the first guy who had the job, Russell was the best chief financial officer we ever had."

That is, aside from the almost $800,000 Russell stole, the $7 million or so authorities say he was preparing to steal, and the $22 million he says he intended to steal from Holmquist and NAMM.

Russell may have been a more engaging conversationalist than the average CFO, but he also had an eye for detail. Soon after starting the job, he noticed that NAMM's internal financial controls were less than rigorous. The most glaring breach of security was the company's use of a rubber signature stamp, rather than a computerized program, for writing and signing checks. Soon after he began working at NAMM, Russell asked that his name be added to the stamp. That idea got shot down. So Russell took matters into his own hands.

"Two days into the job," he says, "I called Vera, the girl who was stamping the checks to go out, into my office and instructed her to copy some documents for me. While she was doing that, I took the signature stamp."

The missing stamp caused a small crisis in the office for the next two days, but company officials decided against replacing the stamp with software.

"In the interim," he says, chuckling, "I was instructed to sign the checks."

He also convinced company officials to add his name to the new signature stamp. The fox had entered the henhouse. Russell immediately closed all of NAMM's accounts at NationsBank, and opened new ones at Texas Commerce Bank.

"I did this so Texas Commerce Bank would appreciate the new business 48 accounts with a balance of $22 million would bring," he says.

While making the transfers, Russell found, to his surprise, that NAMM had been doing nothing to make extra income off the millions that the company routinely deposited.

"They never invested the $22 million they received each month in short-term accounts for the seven to ten days they held the money before disbursing it to the various doctors," he says.

To remedy this squandered opportunity, Russell immediately set up a new account called NAMM Investors. He also opened a parallel account with Chase Securities without bothering to notify anyone else in the company. Each month, Russell would transfer $22 million into the interest-bearing NAMM Investors account, buy stocks with the profits, and then, after seven days, sell them. He then split the resulting revenue 50-50 between himself and his employers, who were none the wiser about the fifty percent commission. In fact, they were quite appreciative of his work.

"NAMM was exceptionally pleased," says Russell, "because before, they were getting nothing, and now they were getting investment income."

While reviewing the company's check register, Russell also discovered that several hundred checks in NAMM's old NationsBank account had never been cashed by their payees. So he had them cleared off the company register, and then transferred the funds directly into the NAMM Investors account, where he could access the money.

"Since these checks had already impacted the plus-and-loss statement as past expenses, no red flags went up," he explains. "Only the balance sheet was affected, and that wasn't noticed by anyone except me."

Russell quickly won respect within the company.

"The guy is the world's best actor," says Holmquist. "He was the ultimate chameleon. He could be whatever he wanted to be. I watched him bossing people around. He was trying to close the books on a particular month. People would come into his office and give him stuff, and it was clear he was in charge. He was their boss. And he fussed at them. He'd say, 'Are you sure these numbers are right?' And I remember thinking, 'This guy's really good.' He said all the right things."

Holmquist concedes that NAMM was extremely care-
less in not running a criminal background check on Russell before hiring him. In the company's defense, he
explains that everyone at NAMM was overworked. If
someone offered to take on even more work and more
responsibilities, there was no reason to say no. When
Russell stepped up to the line, willing to do more than
his share, NAMM officials were thrilled.

It was Russell's grandiose lifestyle that first raised eye-
brows, if not red flags, at the company. He bragged that he
had made a 20 percent down payment on a $107,500 patio
home near the Johnson Space Center. While remodeling,
he and Morris spent $16,000 on a sliding glass door. They
bought matching jet skis, two top-shelf Rolexes, and a
$20,000 Cartier watch. Their conspicuous consumption
also included two 1996 Mercedes-Benzes: a $102,000 SL
500 for Morris and an $86,000 S420 for Russell.

"Everyone at NAMM thought it a little strange when
Steve came in to work one day with a brand new Mercedes," says Holmquist.

Company officials also found it odd that Russell refused
to introduce them to his fiancée, whom he claimed was a
woman who worked for a large Houston law firm.

Meanwhile, Russell and Morris began shopping around
for an even more fashionable home. Their hunt centered

in the exclusive Houston neighborhoods of River Oaks and South Hampton, where the price of even a modest home started at around half a million dollars.

In April 1996, NAMM's CEO, Jeff Rothenberger, offered to sell Russell a townhouse as an investment for $60,000. Russell agreed to buy the property, and applied for a loan from Texas Commerce Bank (TCB), which handled his personal accounts—including a joint checking account with Morris—as well as all of NAMM's accounts.

"Like a fool, I decided to finance it rather than pay cash, which prompted TCB to review my bank statements," he says. "At least I should have used a different bank."

While running routine checks in connection with Russell's loan application—something that most people who crossed paths with Russell never bothered to do—a Texas Commerce loan officer noticed that Russell had an unusually large amount of money in his bank account. The loan officer mentioned it to Chris Grice, the bank official who handled NAMM's account. After a close look at the numbers, Grice realized that during the five previous months, Russell had siphoned off almost $800,000 from NAMM and deposited the money into his personal accounts. Grice made the discovery on May 10, 1996, a Friday, but was unable to notify NAMM officials until Monday, May 13—the fourth anniversary of Russell's first escape from the Harris County Jail.

On Monday, May 13, Russell arrived at work and was surprised to find chief executive officer Jeff Rothenberger there. The CEO usually worked out of the company's Nashville office. Russell walked past Rothenberger's door a couple of times when Rothenberger was on the phone, and overheard enough of his conversation to realize that someone from Texas Commerce Bank was on the other end. He also caught a glimpse of a series of figures that Rothenberger had written on a legal pad.

After Rothenberger hung up, Russell entered his office and invited the CEO to lunch. Rothenberger declined, saying that he had a noon appointment outside the office with an accountant who was working on his income tax return. But he made a point of telling Russell that he needed to see him that afternoon.

"Jeff could never be a poker player," muses Russell, "because I sensed a dramatic change in his demeanor after the phone call. I knew he was lying because he had already told me that he does his own taxes every year. So I definitely knew that something was up."

As soon as Rothenberger left the building, Russell slipped into Rothenberger's office. He found the legal pad, but Rothenberger had taken the top sheet on which he'd written the series of figures. Undaunted, Russell employed an old detectives' trick, using a pencil to lightly trace the indentations left on the notepad. The numbers

Rothenberger had written on the pad loosely corresponded with the money Russell had embezzled.

Russell sprang into action. First, he checked the briefcase Rothenberger had left behind. Russell knew that Rothenberger never locked his briefcase, but this time he had. Russell then calmly walked back to his own office, packed up a few items, and shredded a few others. Before leaving the building, he ducked back into Rothenberger's office, grabbed the briefcase, and walked out the front door. Next, he drove to a hardware store, bought a screwdriver, and pried open the briefcase. Judging by the documents and notes inside, Rothenberger had just begun his investigation. Russell also noted that Rothenberger had an appointment the following day at the Harris County district attorney's office.

Russell emptied the briefcase into an industrial garbage bin in back of the hardware store. On his mobile phone, he called Morris's friend Duane Nowell, whom Russell had helped get a low-level job at NAMM, for a briefing on the current atmosphere at the office.

"Rothenberger's looking for you," said Nowell. "Everybody's looking for you. They're all asking me where you are, and why you haven't come back from lunch."

Russell gave Nowell the lowdown. He wasn't coming back from lunch. He wasn't coming back at all. And since Russell had instructed Nowell to lie on his job application to NAMM and say that he, too, had worked for Prudential, Nowell knew he wouldn't be coming back, either.

Russell also called Phillip Morris. To this day Russell insists that Morris had no knowledge that he was embezzling money from NAMM, that he intentionally kept Morris uninformed. Sure, Russell deposited some of the money into the checking account he shared with Morris, and Morris withdrew money from that account. But, Russell says, Morris never suspected the money had been stolen. According to Russell, only when his operation was discovered did he reveal to Morris the source of the funds that had allowed them to live so lavishly. Prosecutors maintain otherwise, claiming that Morris actively took part in the scheme.

Either way, Morris was none too pleased when Russell called on his cell phone to break the news.

"Why did you do this, Steve?" he asked. "You said you weren't going to do this kind of thing anymore. I can't believe you."

"I'm sorry," said Russell.

"You're sorry?" Morris replied. "Well, that's not good enough. I'm leaving. Now. Before they come after me, too."

chapter eleven

The Great Escape

After his abrupt phone conversation with Morris, Russell continued driving toward his house in southeast Houston. He was scared—not about being discovered by NAMM, although that concerned him, but about losing Morris. He had to get home before Morris left. This did not prevent him, however, from stopping at several ATMs along the way, withdrawing as much cash as he could at each stop from each of his bank accounts.

As he drove down the freeway, his cell phone rang. He wasn't going to answer, but then thought that it might be Morris calling him back.

"Hello," he answered.

"Steve?" said the voice on the other end. It wasn't Phillip.

"Yeah, who is this?"

"Steve, this is Don Holmquist. I'm here at the office. We were sort of looking for you when you didn't come back from lunch. Where are you?"

"I'm on the Gulf Freeway," replied Russell. Why he uncharacteristically told Holmquist the truth, he wasn't sure.

"Well, when are you going to be back?" asked Holmquist. "We need to talk with you about something."

"Do you really think I should come back? Maybe I just won't come back at all."

"I think you should come back, because we really need to talk."

"Don't worry, Don," Russell said. "My attorney will be in touch."

With that, Russell pushed the phone's off button, rolled down the Mercedes's window, and tossed the phone out onto the freeway.

Implausible as it may sound, Russell insists that he really did intend to have his lawyer work out some sort of deal with NAMM—specifically, a deal that would not involve criminal charges. His past experiences indicated that NAMM wouldn't care, or dare, to bring charges against him. Most likely, he thought, company brass would prefer to work out a deal quietly with his attorney to get a portion of the money back, rather than file charges and reveal publicly that they had hired an impostor to handle their finances.

By the time Russell pulled up to his house, Morris was gone. Russell tried reaching him by calling his friends, to no avail. The next day, Russell's persistence paid off.

"My sister called me, and got me to come over to her house [in Houston]," Morris recalls. "And when I got there, Steve was sitting on the sofa."

Next to Russell lay a briefcase containing $40,000, part of the previous day's ATM withdrawals. Russell shoved the briefcase toward Morris.

"Here, this is yours."

"No, it is not," said Morris. "It's not my money."

"Where'd you get that money?" demanded Morris's sister, Pam Beckham, an attractive, tall brunette. "I've never seen that much money!"

Russell continued to insist that Morris take the cash. Morris continued to refuse. Finally, Beckham agreed to take the money to Russell's ex-wife, Debbie, in Virginia. Debbie then turned it over to her attorney, who sent it back to Texas law enforcement officials. Harris County officials confirm her version of events. Russell apparently had Debbie figured wrong. At least this time.

Debbie Russell balks when asked to speak candidly

about why she, a devout Christian, remains loyal to her gay, con artist ex-husband. But Steven and Debbie's daughter, Stephanie Russell, who is now 23, says that deep down, both she and her mother believe that Steven Russell is a kind, decent man who, in his own way, has tried to be a good father, friend, and provider.

"I know he's done some bad things," says Stephanie, who, like her mother, asked me not to reveal where they work or what they do. "But that doesn't mean that he's a bad man, or that we'd don't still love him."

After all these years, anytime Steven Russell finds himself in trouble, which happens quite often, he knows he can still call on Debbie to help him. And she usually does.

"People have been unfair to him," says Debbie, defiantly, after much prodding. "He was never mean to me. He never mistreated me. And so who does he have left to be there for him now? I just can't walk away. I'm not that coldhearted. But if people think I've profited from what he's done, they can take a look around. There's nothing here. They'd be lucky to find some loose change in the couch."

H. P. Williams, Russell's cousin, however, has something of an insider's view into the relationship between Steven and Debbie. A former district attorney, Williams now lives and practices law in Elizabeth City, North Carolina. At various times, he has represented both Steven and Debbie. Williams believes Debbie, much like Phillip, remains loyal to Steven because of the attention he pays to her.

"I believe that Steve, in his own way, makes those around him feel extra special," says Williams. "Debbie is very needy. Steve makes her feel needed. She is also very naïve. She believes anything Steve tells her. I've had to yell at her to get her to listen to reason."

Terry Jennings, a former Harris County assistant district attorney, now an appellate judge in Texas, came to know both Russell and Morris well, and has his own interpretation.

"I think she [remains loyal to Russell] because she has so much invested in him emotionally," Jennings says. "It's like they say about a good salesman. If he spends enough time with you, he can get you to buy something. A con man is a salesman of sorts. Debbie and Stephanie have so much of Steven wrapped up in their psyche, they don't want to believe he's a crook. They want to help him. They want to believe him. They want to take his side. And I have to admit, after a while, even I came to view him somewhat as this lovable rogue."

And in the aftermath of NAMM, Russell was his roguish best.

To Steven Russell's surprise, the day after his hasty departure from the NAMM offices, the Harris County district attorney's office launched an investigation of him and the $800,000 missing from NAMM's accounts. Jeff Rothenberger, the company's CEO, met with Maria McAnulty, the district attorney's special crimes division chief. McAnulty assigned the case to Terry Jennings, who at the time still worked as an assistant district attorney for Harris County. Baby-faced, with fair skin, sandy hair, and glasses, Jennings is a congenial fellow with a taste for politics, courtroom convictions, and the jugular.

After learning that Russell was probably on the run, Jennings accelerated the investigation. Given Russell's background in escape and fraud, Jennings knew his suspect might be clever enough to inquire about the status of the investigation. A series of unusual phone calls to various Harris County offices soon confirmed his suspicions.

At the request of the district attorney's office, state District Judge Mary Bacon signed an order freezing Russell's and Morris's assets. A few days later, Bacon received a call from someone claiming to be a federal judge from Virginia.

"How're you doing, Judge?" Bacon drawled.

"Well, Judge, I've got a little project I'm working on, and I wanted to see if you could help me with it," the voice replied. "I'm working on a paper that has to do with the rights of prisoners with AIDS. And I've been putting this question to a lot of judges around the country. What I'd like to know is this: Do you think that prisoners with AIDS, do you think those prisoners should receive lighter sentences than other felons? I would like to know how you deal with those people in your sentencing scheme."

"Well, Texas doesn't have sentencing guidelines," said Bacon. "The judges and prosecutors have the flexibility to deal with the nuances of each case."

When a federal judge calls you on the phone, you pay attention and try to be helpful, even if you are a judge yourself. Bacon listened patiently to the questions for a few minutes. But the more she listened, the more the queries began to smell peculiar.

"Say a person has advanced HIV, and is charged with a nonviolent criminal offense," asked the caller. "What would be the maximum or minimum sentence imposed?"

A crusty and experienced jurist, Bacon quickly brought the conversation to an end, and promptly notified Jennings and the district attorney's office about the strange call. Jennings assumed—correctly—that it was Russell who had called Bacon. If Russell had the gumption to call a judge and impersonate another judge, Jennings figured that his suspect would probably feel free to make other calls, including, most likely, some to the Harris County district clerk's office.

In a typical criminal probe by the district attorney's office, prosecutors first conduct a thorough investigation, and then file charges. Those charges are then recorded with the district clerk's office, and a judge issues a warrant for the suspect's arrest—even before the facts of the case are presented to a grand jury. So far, no formal charges had been filed against Russell. For the time being, Jennings intended to keep it that way. Russell could monitor the progress of the investigation by periodically calling the district clerk's office under some bogus pretext to see if charges had been filed against him, or if a warrant had been issued for his arrest. But Jennings threw Russell a curve by obtaining what is known as a pocket warrant.

"We drafted an arrest warrant and had a judge sign it," Jennings says. "But we didn't file it with the clerk's office." With no record of a warrant having been issued, Jennings had a hunch his suspect might feel secure enough to return to his home. It was a good guess.

Two investigators from the DA's office took the warrant and watched Russell's house. Sure enough, on May 23, ten days after bolting from NAMM, Russell stopped by to pick up a few things. The investigators picked him up instead.

"And one of the first things he said when he was arrested," says Jennings, "was, 'Damn pocket warrants! Y'all haven't used those in ten or twelve years!' Otherwise, he would have never gone back to his house."

Russell had been outsmarted this time, but even as he was being arrested, he found a wild card to play.

"Hey, fellas," he said as the detectives were helping him into the backseat. "I'm a diabetic. That's the reason I came back here, to get my insulin. And I need to take it right now. You don't want me going into insulin shock on you before we get to the jail, do you?"

The veteran detectives looked at each other and rolled their eyes. Without saying anything, they led Russell into the house and to the bathroom. In one of the drawers next to the bathroom sink, they found a packet of syringes and needles, and a prescription bottle of insulin. Apparently the detectives didn't notice that the label on the bottle indicated the insulin had been prescribed for Phillip Morris.

Not waiting for questions, he quickly attached a needle to a syringe, inserted it into the insulin bottle, pulled back the plunger, and then jammed the needle into his arm.

"You sure do take a lot of insulin," one of the detectives commented. Indeed he did. In fact, Russell went through the entire vial, and he estimates that he gave himself approximately 40 injections on the drive back downtown, as well as in the DA's office while being interviewed. When the questioning ended, Russell was taken to the Harris County Jail nearby. There, during the booking process, he went into insulin shock and passed out. An ambulance transported him to LBJ Hospital. A few days later, when he recovered, he went directly back to the county jail.

Why the insulin stunt? Jennings calls Russell's intentional overdose a diversionary ploy to give him the time to find a way to escape. Russell insists he was trying to kill himself, grief-stricken over involving Morris in the NAMM affair.

In fact, prosecutors did suspect that Morris was complicit in the embezzling scheme. Some of the NAMM money had been improperly transferred through checks written to "P. C. Morris" and "Dr. Morris, P.C." It didn't take much else to convince the DA's office that Phillip Clark Morris was involved up to his ears in the scam.

In an attempt to convince prosecutors of his innocence, Morris tape recorded a telephone conversation he had with Russell. It took place while Morris was still on the run and Russell was incarcerated in the Harris County lock-up. Prosecutors believe the conversation was staged, but Russell and Morris both deny it.

"I don't want to hurt you," says Russell, as the tape begins. "You know I wouldn't..."

"Well, you've already hurt me, Steve," Morris interrupts, sounding a bit like a foul-mouthed Southern belle drama queen in a Tennessee Williams play. "You got me drug into this goddamn mess. And I told you not to do anything wrong. I told you. And you promised me that you wouldn't do anything like this. You promised. You promised me that we would never wind up back in jail. And now that's where I'm goddamn headed again. For something I didn't do. And you know I didn't know about it. You know I didn't know anything about this."

"And I told the district attorney that I know that you didn't," Russell replies in a shaky voice. "They're trying to get you into my mess. What they're trying to do is to get you to turn against me."

"No, Steve, they don't do that, try to turn somebody against somebody. They would call me. They would subpoena me to court if they were trying to get to you. You know that as well as I do."

"No," says Russell. "No."

"You've taken me for a fool!" Morris interrupts again. "You've used me, Steve. You've used me."

"No, I didn't."

"Yes, you have used me, Steve. You knew with my name on that checking account, that it would tie me in to you. Now, I told you not to do anything, Steve. I begged you not to do anything to jeopardize our freedom. You know how important my freedom is to me. I'm thinking about committing suicide, I'm so fucking nervous!"

When Morris surrendered two days after his dramatic

conversation took place, the recording had little sway on the DA's office. The prosecutors gave greater weight to the joint checking account that Morris had with Russell, and the $102,000 check Morris wrote on that account to purchase his Mercedes-Benz.

"Sure, he was angry," Jennings says of Morris. "He was angry that Steven got caught. But of course Phillip knew about it. Phillip signed one of the damn checks. He knew Steven was on parole. And Phillip knew that you don't get a job as CFO of a company while you're on parole for insurance fraud."

Nevertheless, Russell insists that entire scheme was his idea and his doing—alone. And he regrets getting Morris caught up in it.

"Causing someone to go to jail for something they didn't do," Russell says, "that's the worst thing in the world you can do. But that's what I caused to happen to Phillip. And I'll never forgive myself."

Eventually, Russell and Morris were both charged with felony theft. Morris was freed pending his trial after friends posted his $40,000 bond. Since Russell was considered a flight risk, however, his bond was set at $900,000. He wouldn't be going anywhere anytime soon. Or so Jennings and other Harris County authorities thought.

Through his attorney, Roger Bridgewater, Russell had a new bond hearing set for July 12, 1996. "I asked Bridgewater to set it for that date," Russell says. "One way or another, I was going to be a free man on the 13th."

Russell hoped that the hearing would result in a reduction of his bond. After all, most murder suspects get lesser bonds, and he was only charged with theft. But he had a back-up plan ready, just in case. If the judge didn't reduce his bond, Russell would have to take matters into his own hands. To his way of thinking, the district attorney's office had left him no choice.

"The prosecutors initially told me that they were going to press for a twenty-year sentence," he explains. "Then they turned around and jumped it up to forty-five years. If this had been a federal case, with good behavior I would have been out in eight years. I could have parked my ass for eight years, no problem. But now I was looking at at least half of the forty-five. When you tell someone that they have to do that much time, they have nothing to lose by escaping. Simple as that!"

Russell knew how the system worked. When a prisoner is processed into county jail, he is accompanied by a warrant or an indictment, which includes the amount of the prisoner's bond. During processing, a deputy enters the bond amount and the inmate's identification number into a computer. When a prisoner's number is pulled up on the computer system, his bond amount also appears, along with his charge, his next court date, and whether there are any warrants or holds on him in any other law enforcement jurisdictions.

Russell hoped to manipulate the system by calling the district clerk's office. He knew that whenever a prisoner in the Harris County Jail makes a call, the operator notifies the person receiving the call that it is a collect call from the jail. To get around this problem, Russell decided he would first place a long-distance call to a friend in Florida with a three-way conference-call connection. The friend would then forward Russell's call back to the Harris County District Clerk's office.

Getting a bond reduction into the system also required a hard copy of the court order stating the new figure. The clerk in each individual court handles this step. Obviously, the clerk in the 177th District Court, in which Russell had been arraigned, would be of no help; Russell had to find a way around her. In his jail cell, he drew a mock-up of the document he needed, and then mailed it to his friend in Florida. The friend had an official-looking version printed up—one that looked like a court order lowering the bond to $45,000—and then sent it back to Russell. Before leaving his cell for his July 12 hearing, Russell hid his counterfeit bond reduction order underneath his jumpsuit.

For the two-block walk from the jail to the old criminal courthouse, Russell and about a dozen other prisoners scheduled to appear that day were handcuffed to a long metal chain and escorted by sheriff's deputies. The journey took them through a labyrinth of tunnels under the county court complex. Along the way, Russell tried to think of how he could plant the bogus document in the court clerk's in-basket, to make it look as if the judge had placed it there. Because he was going directly to a holding cell located behind the courtroom, he couldn't put it there himself.

As he and his fellow prisoners paused in a subterranean hallway to wait for an elevator, Russell noticed a woman with a large bundle of files and documents approaching. When she walked past, he slipped his homemade court order out of his pants, and let it drop onto the hallway floor. When the woman was just out of earshot, Russell got the attention of one of the deputies, then reached down and picked up the fake document.

"Hey deputy," he yelled. "I think that woman that just walked by dropped this. I hollered at her, but she just kept walking."

"Lemme have that," the deputy snarled, snatching the paper from Russell's hand. "I'll drop it off in the district clerk's office." Exactly what Russell wanted to hear.

During his bond hearing, just as Russell had suspected, things did not go well. Although the judge cut his bond in half to $450,000, the prosecutor hit Russell with a second charge of misapplication of funds, for which the judge set a second bond, also for $450,000. In effect, the total bond remained at $900,000.

After their hearings, Russell and the rest of the chain gang were herded back to their cells. By mid-afternoon, jail officials notified Russell that he had received a copy of his bond reduction—the one he had forged. Now he had to work fast. If he wasn't released by 1:00 A.M.—the cutoff time for the discharge of prisoners—he'd have to wait until the next morning. By then, the real paperwork might arrive and they'd be on to him.

That evening, on a phone designated for inmate use, Russell called his Florida accomplice, who patched him back through to Houston and the district clerk's office. The phone rang, and a female voice answered.

"District clerk's office."

"Yes, hello, this is Judge Charles Hearn," said Russell. (Hearn was an actual retired judge who occasionally filled in for vacationing jurists.) "I'm serving as visiting judge in the 177th. I had a bond hearing for a Steven Russell earlier today, and I made a mistake on the bond amount. Instead of $450,000 on each charge, it should be $22,500. I've already sent a hard copy of the order over to the jail. I just need for you to make the change in the computer records."

That was that. Now all he needed was a bail bondsman. Another patched-through conference call hooked
him up with A-Rose Bonding Company in Houston.
This time Russell posed as his attorney.

"A-Rose," a man answered.

"Hi there, this is Roger Bridgewater. I represent Steven
Russell, who's being held at the 1301 Franklin jail. Judge
Hearn gave him a bond reduction today, and I sure
would like to get him bonded out before the weekend. I'll
stand behind the bond myself, and I'll get the money to
you on Monday."

Two hours later, the deputy in charge of the cell floor
told Russell to pack his bags.

On hand to greet Russell in the jail's public lobby was
the bonding agent who'd posted his bail.

"You Russell?"

"Yeah, who are you?"

"I'm from A-Rose. Bridgewater called us."

"Thanks," Russell said, trying not to laugh.

"No problem."

"Hey, do you think you could do me another favor?"
asked Russell, pushing his luck.

"What's that?"

"Well, I live all the way down by the space center. I
mean, it's already after midnight. I don't have any way to

get home. Could you give me a ride? I'll make sure Roger gives you something extra on Monday."

Half an hour later, they arrived at Russell's house. Since he had no keys to unlock the front gate, and their was no doorbell on the gate, he had to scale the six-foot brick wall to get inside his compound.

Morris was home. With the help of friends, he had made his bond—legally. Russell told him he had made bail, too. He didn't explain how. Even though he knew he had only a limited amount of time before his scam was discovered, Russell jumped in the pool, swam for two hours, and took a short nap. When he awoke, he made a proposition to Morris.

"Let's go to Florida."

"We can't go to Florida, Steve. We can't even leave the county."

"Of course, we can. We can do whatever we want to do. We'll go underground just like Jimmy and I did. We can do this."

Morris wasn't buying it. True, Russell and his previous boyfriend, Jimmy Kemple, had outrun authorities from several states and the federal government for a couple years. But where had it gotten them? In the end, Russell had gone to jail, and Kemple was dead. Morris was not yet ready to play Bonnie to Russell's Clyde.

In that case, Russell said he would rent a trailer and

move his furniture into storage under an alias. He would have it shipped to Florida when he decided where he was going to settle. In turn, Morris told Russell he would get his own apartment, and join him in Florida after his trial was over and he was declared innocent.

After breakfast, the two drove to downtown Houston so Morris could check in with his bondsman, and then spent some time looking at apartments for Morris. That night, they stayed home and watched TV. There was no news of Russell's escape. Sunday morning, Morris packed his belongings, planning to room with a friend in Galveston until he found his own place. Russell hired two guys from Home Depot to load his furniture into a rented trailer and haul it to storage.

The more Russell thought about going to Florida without Morris, though, the less he liked it. He knew the authorities would wait for him to contact or eventually return for Morris. He decided he had to convince Morris that running away was his best choice.

Russell called the district clerk's office and told the woman who answered the phone that he was Deputy Johnson with the Harris County sheriff's office, and that he needed her help to play a trick on a friend, Phillip Morris. He said that when he called her back, he wanted her to confirm for Morris that a blue warrant—a warrant for someone who has violated parole—had been issued for his arrest. The clerk agreed.

"I felt like a big creep for tricking Phillip," Russell says. "And I regret not being candid with Phillip when we first met. My lack of candor was based on the reality of a prison romance's chance of survival. Usually it doesn't work. But the bond that ties us together is incredibly strong and has only intensified. There isn't anything I wouldn't do for him."

When Morris called the clerk's office, he panicked. Against his better judgment, he agreed to go to Florida. He felt as if he had run out of options.

The two men decided it would be safer if they traveled separately. They agreed to meet up at the bus station on Broward Boulevard in Fort Lauderdale on July 18 at 10:00 A.M. Morris would travel by bus. Russell would drive their pickup.

On his way to Florida, Russell contacted his ex-wife's lawyer and asked him to wire him the $40,000 he had shipped to Debbie. The attorney wouldn't hear of it. But he did agree to wire the money to another attorney, if Russell could find one who would turn around and give it to him. He couldn't.

"I should have given up on the fucking money," says Russell. "Phillip had $4,000, and I had $3,000. That would have been enough for us to get an apartment and get started. No, I had to get greedy."

On Tuesday night, Russell checked in to the Red Roof Inn on 45th Street in West Palm Beach. Furious about the attorney's refusal to hand over the money, he called Debbie. In retrospect, Russell believes that by that time Harris County authorities had tapped Debbie's phone.

About one o'clock Wednesday morning, Russell heard someone banging on his motel door and yelling "Fire!"

"That's an old cop trick," Russell says. "I used it myself."

Russell knew what was going down. So he called Helen Kemple, Jimmy's mother, who lived nearby, and told her to warn Phillip. Phillip knew to call Helen if he couldn't find Russell.

"After that," Russell says, "I opened the door and I was arrested."

Morris stuck to the plan and eventually made it to Fort Lauderdale, where he heard about Russell's arrest. He began the long trip back to Houston. Alone.

chapter twelve

The Greater Escape

In the summer of 1996, more than four years after Russell's first trip to the Harris County Jail, Russell was again heading back there after having been captured at the Red Roof Inn in West Palm Beach. He had plenty of company on his return trip to Houston: three armed deputies from Harris County's fugitive warrants division. Upon his arrival in Houston, Captain Dan Doehring of the Harris County sheriff's office was there to welcome Russell back when he and his pistol-packing entourage arrived at the jail in an unmarked car.

"If Steve Russell tells you the sun is shining," warns Captain Doehring, "I suggest you go outside and see for yourself if that big yellow thing that hurts your eyes is in the sky."

Doehring was the sheriff's ranking officer overseeing the jail, and Russell had burned him twice. He was determined not to let it happen again. Doehring ordered his jailers to place Russell in arm and leg shackles anytime he was moved from his cell. He also prohibited Russell from any unsupervised use of the telephones. Indeed, Terry Jennings, the former Harris County prosecutor, thinks that it was the phone restrictions, more than the shackles, that led Russell to quickly plead guilty to his $800,000 embezzlement from North American Medical Management, for which he was sentenced to 45 years in state prison. "Steven is a master manipulator of the telephone," Jennings says. "So when we cut off his access, he pled out pretty fast, despite the length of the sentence. Because I don't think he ever had any intention of serving it. He just wanted to get to wherever he was going in the Texas Department of Criminal Justice, so he could start working on his next escape."

He didn't even want to wait that long. While confined in Harris County Jail and awaiting transfer to a state facility in August 1996, during a recreation—the one time during the day when he was not shackled—Russell hopped into an elevator with a janitor and tried to pass himself off as a member of the cleaning crew. This time he got caught. The next month, he was sent back to TDCJ to begin serving his 45 years.

Usually, when an inmate gets transferred from Harris County Jail to state prison, he rides to Huntsville with a large group of prisoners on a secure bus. Harris County deputies transported Russell by car, all by himself. During the handover, the deputies made a point of stressing to their state counterparts that Russell had a history of escape, and that they should monitor his activities closely. The warning apparently went unheeded.

If Steven Russell were to teach a course called Escape 101, he says, he would first tell his students that the least spectacular method of escape always works best.

"This bullshit about getting out and laying low for 72 hours, or hiding out nearby until the heat dies down, is pure garbage, and it will get you caught," he says. "Planning is the key."

In October, after passing through Huntsville's inmate processing unit, Russell was assigned to the Estelle Unit, about ten miles north of the city. As soon as he arrived, he immediately scouted for the least noticeable way out. He saw four options: (1) walk out the front door, dressed as either a maintenance worker or a doctor; (2) cut his way out of his cell, climbing out the window and using wire cutters to breach the perimeter fence; (3) obtain a special parole; or (4) impersonate a trusty and leave on a trash truck (harking back to his childhood ambition to become a garbage man). He decided on Option No. 1, which as a bonus would make TDCJ look foolish.

To walk out the front gate of Estelle Unit, Russell would need new clothes. Keeping civilian clothes or a uniform might draw suspicion, possibly tempting someone to snitch on him. It would also be too similar to his recent "red pants" escape. He had to find clothing that he could keep in his cell legitimately, but that he could also alter. To perform the needed reconnaissance work, he faked some eye trouble and was sent to the prison's medical facility, operated by the University of Texas Medical Branch, or UTMB, inside Estelle Unit. As soon as he arrived, Russell swiped a medical pass and wrote his name on it. He then began walking around the hospital, observing how people were dressed, and how they left the facility. He noticed that a dialysis patient wore a white shirt that resembled surgical scrubs, with "UTMB" stenciled on the front.

Bingo. Russell told an inmate named Sean who worked in the hospital that he needed one of the shirts to sleep in.

"It'll cost you a three-dollar bag of coffee," Sean said.

"Just get it," Russell replied.

Russell thought that prison pants could pass for surgical-scrubs bottoms, so he placed an order with another inmate for a fresh pair. This cost him one dollar. But Russell knew that white scrubs would not get him out the front gate. Inmate patients wore white scrubs. Doctors wore green scrubs. He looked for dye in the prison crafts shop, but couldn't find any that was water-based. The shop had paint but that wouldn't look right. Then, Russell noticed an inmate drawing with a Magic Marker.

"Can I buy one of those green ones from you?" he asked.

"Sure. Fifty cents apiece."

Russell began to test his dye on scraps of cloth. Placing the marker in a full sink and then soaking the fabric in the water seemed to work best. At every opportunity, he purchased more markers, four or five at a time. While surveying the prison, he noticed that a young female guard usually manned the front door checkpoint to his unit from ten at night to six in the morning. She seemed inexperienced and lackadaisical. Just the qualities he was looking for.

"More than unorganized, she was lazy, lazy, lazy," says Russell. "Otherwise, [the escape] wouldn't have happened."

It was early December, and Friday the 13th was approaching. Just a few days before he planned to make his move, prison officials unintentionally threw a hitch into Russell's scheme by assigning him a roommate. Worse, the man almost never left the cell except to perform his job cleaning the prison showers. When the time came to move, Russell would have to move fast.

On December 12, Russell stayed in his cell all day. As soon as his cellmate left for work, Russell hurriedly dyed his extra clothes in a sink full of green marker water. He tried using his cellmate's electric box fan to dry them, but it was taking too long.

"I ended up putting them in between two blankets, and laid down on them," he says.

Around 3:00 A.M., just before the prison's ungodly early breakfast, he slipped into his disguise, then put his white prison uniform and green prison jacket on over it. After breakfast, he entered a restroom near the psychological evaluation office, shed his prison whites, and stepped out into the hallway. Right away he was face to face with an inmate who recognized him. For a second, Russell feared the worst.

"Wow," the inmate said. "Good luck."

Russell hurried down the hallway, past the captain's office, past the female guard's vacant checkpoint, and out the front door. A short walk later, he reached the outer gate and waited for the guard on duty to open it.

"Man, your clothes look like prison whites, Doc," the guard said.

"Well, don't shoot me," Russell replied, trying to appear nonchalant.

The guard laughed. "No, Doc, I was just kidding."

The front gate opened. Russell was on his way. He laughed silently to himself.

Although the sun hadn't yet risen, it was Friday the 13th, and he had done it again.

Outside the perimeter of any Texas prison, it's easy for someone—say, an escaped convict—not familiar with area to get disoriented. The facilities are located where they are located for a reason. But it was a cool, clear morning, and Russell took his directional bearings from the stars. After what felt like forever, he reached the main road. For a rural two-lane blacktop, there seemed to be a lot of traffic at such an early hour. Had a manhunt already begun? Making his way along the road, Russell stayed close to the trees and fence line, and low to the ground. After a few hundred yards, he dared to cross the road. Just then, a fast-approaching pickup truck bore down on him. Russell dove into the grass and lay flat and still. The truck's brake lights came on. The driver began steering the vehicle into a U-turn. Russell quickly crossed the road and dashed into the woods.

Working his way through trees and underbrush for half an hour or so, he came upon a house in a clearing. Going for broke, Russell rang the bell, knocked on the door, and prepared to tell a story. A few moments later, a man slowly opened the door. His hands were behind his back. Russell attempted a disarming smile.

"Sorry to bother you at this hour," he said, grinning. "I'm a TDCJ doctor, and I just wrecked my car. Ran it off into a ditch on the way out of the unit. I'd call back to the office for help, but I got to confess to you, I've been drinking. I'm a little bit drunk. If you could help me get back into town, I could take care of this before anybody finds out. If the cops get involved I could lose my medical license, so I sure would appreciate your help."

"You sure look bad, son," the man said. "Come on in and I'll get you a cup of coffee."

"I don't drink coffee, but I sure could use a glass of water," said Russell, relieved. Ushering Russell into his living room, the man ducked into the kitchen to get water for Russell and a cup of coffee for himself. Russell gulped it down.

"Do you want another?" the man asked.

"No, but thanks a lot. I just really need to get to Huntsville before somebody finds my car."

The two got into the man's car and headed down the road to Huntsville in the dark. During the 10-mile ride, the man, whose name was Bobby Rushing, told Russell a little about himself and his wife. "She's a secretary for the prison system," he said. "She works over there at the administration building."

"I guess a lot of us around here work for the prison," said Russell, straining to remain calm.

"But she's sick," Rushing continued. "She's got MS."

"If you'll write to me, I'll send you some information on MS," Russell said.

Rushing handed him a notepad and pen. "Here, write your name and address on this."

Figuring it would be a while before he actually got around to looking at the notepad, Russell wrote his name as "Dr. C. U. Later."

"Thanks," said Rushing. "I'll be in touch."

"Please do," said Russell.

Soon, the car approached a Denny's—the same one where Russell and Morris had laughed about Morris's early release a year earlier. "You can just drop me off here," said Russell. "I can call for some help from inside. Thanks a lot for helping me out."

"No problem," said Rushing. "Good luck with your car."

Inside Denny's, Russell used the restaurant's phone to call a cab. The minutes crawled by. Russell wondered if his keepers at Estelle Unit had noticed his absence yet. Finally, a cab pulled into the lot, and he walked out to greet it. He and his fake surgical scrubs were covered with dirt and sweat, but he couldn't stop now.

He opened a rear door and slid into the backseat. The license attached near the cab's meter identified the driver as Margie Allen.

"Where to?" asked Allen, an amiable black woman.

"Well, this may be a little unusual," said Russell, "but I need you to drive me down to Hermann Hospital in the medical center in Houston."

"That's about seventy-five miles, Mister."

"I know, but it's sort of an emergency. I'm a doctor over at the Estelle Unit. I was drinking on duty last night, and I ran off the road and wrecked my car when I was leaving the unit this morning. And I just realized I left my wallet at Hermann when I was working down there yesterday. So I need to get down there in hurry so I can get my wallet and deal with my car before the police find it."

"Well, all right then."

During the drive, Allen and Russell chatted, sharing their opinions about current events. They learned that they both opposed the death penalty. Allen also told Russell about her own brush with death months earlier.

"One time I picked up this fare who turned out to be an escapee," she said. "After he got into the cab, he put a knife to my throat. But I just drove him to where he wanted to go, and he got out."

"You must have been scared to death," replied Russell.

"You got that right."

After about 90 minutes, they reached Texas Medical Center, just south of downtown Houston.

"Where do you want me to go?" asked Allen.

"Just pull into the emergency driveway there behind

Hermann Hospital. I'll go in and get my wallet, and then come back out and pay you."

"Okay," she said, guiding the taxi toward the entrance to the emergency room. "That'll be $125."

"That's fine," said Russell, exiting the cab.

"Hey there, what do you think you're doing?" a voice boomed. It came from a man in a uniform, and Russell's heart raced. But it was just a security guard.

"You can't park there!" the guard continued. "This area is restricted to emergency vehicles. We got ambulances coming in and out of here. You're going to have move that cab."

"This is an emergency, officer," said Russell. "I'm a doctor here, and I'm late for surgery. But I need to go in and get my wallet so I can pay this lady. Can't she just park here while I run inside?"

"All right, go ahead. Just don't be too long."

"I'll be right back," Russell promised.

Inside the hospital, Russell moved quickly.

"Which way to surgery?" he asked another security guard in the lobby.

"Second floor."

Russell took the elevator there, and approached a nurse.

"Excuse me, ma'am," he said. "I'm a doctor with UTMB.

I've just had car trouble, and I really need a change of clothes."

"Sure," the nurse said, and she led him to a supply closet filled with fresh surgical scrubs.

"You're welcome to use our showers if you want to," she said.

"No, thanks," he answered. "I'm already late enough as it is."

In a restroom, Russell donned his fresh scrubs, then hurried out of the hospital and briskly walked north on Main Street to an old Sears store where he knew there was a taxi stand. There he caught another cab, which took him another couple of miles to Carriage Car Care, in Montrose. The part-owner of that business, Craig Dees, had briefly shared an apartment with Russell in the mid-1980s. He knew nothing of Russell's escape.

After catching his breath for a few minutes, Russell phoned both his ex-wife Debbie and Helen Kemple, Jimmy's mother. He didn't tell them he had escaped, but convinced each of them to wire him $250. By nine that morning, the money had arrived. Dees drove Russell to a supermarket to pick up the cash, then the old friends went to a Mexican restaurant for an early lunch. Russell, who by this point in his life rarely drank much, downed several margaritas. After all, you don't break out of state prison every day.

After lunch, Dees dropped him off back at Sears, where Russell bought some new clothes. Then he caught a bus all the way out to Clear Lake, the end of the line. From there, he hailed another cab for the 20-mile trip to the southern end of Interstate 45, at Galveston Island. Twenty miles that would lead him to his reunion with Phillip Morris.

Since making bail the previous summer, Morris had been living on Galveston Island with a friend named Scott English, waiting to be tried on the theft charges filed against him in connection with the missing NAMM money. Instead of going directly to English's house, Russell had the cabdriver drop him off at the beach. He spent the next few hours sunning himself, wanting to lose his unhealthy prison pallor before seeing Morris. After sunset, he walked to a spot a couple of blocks from English's home, and spent a long while studying the house to make sure the police didn't have it under surveillance. Nothing seemed out of the ordinary. Around eight o'clock, when Morris stepped out of the house, he made his move. "Surprise!" he yelled.

Morris wheeled around and laughed. "Honey, this is no surprise," he said.

"I've got a calendar, and I know what day it is. I've been expecting you."

Giggling wildly, the two men embraced on the sidewalk.

"So, where are we going?" asked Russell

"Where do you want to go?" replied Morris.

"Any place besides where I've been lately."

After a few giddy moments, it occurred to Russell that they should get off the street and out of sight. Inside, they weighed their travel options, and soon decided on Florida. Russell knew the turf, and he could get work and still stay underground. They decided to have English drive them across the Texas border to Lake Charles, Louisiana, where they would spend the night. About three hours later, around midnight, English dropped the two off at a motel and quickly slipped away, hoping to avoid getting caught up in the trouble he feared his friends were heading for. Russell and Morris went straight to bed.

The next morning, Russell rose early, dressed, and walked to a nearby restaurant to bring back food for breakfast in bed. In the restaurant's foyer he saw several coin-operated newspaper boxes, including one for the *Houston Chronicle*. There in the box, staring back at him, was one of his own mug shots, accompanied by an article about his escape. Russell put two quarters in the machine, opened the spring-hinged door, pulled out a paper, and began to read.

"Investigators familiar with his tactics expected

smooth-talking Steven Russell to escape from prison," the story began. "It was just a matter of time. The most prolific jail escapee in Harris County history worked his magic again Friday morning, walking out of his state prison unit near Huntsville dressed in what appeared to be physician scrubs. 'We warned them. We told [TDCJ officials] this guy is going to escape from prison,' said Dan McAnulty, an investigator for the [Harris County] district attorney's office."

Russell continued to skim the article until he came to a quote that made him burst out laughing.

"Obviously some [security] things broke down, and we will look at those things," said [TDCJ spokesman] David Nunnelee.

"Obviously," Russell said to himself.

But he didn't laugh long. He knew that TDCJ's fugitive trackers, as well as law-enforcement officers from Texas and probably several other states, were hunting for him, and perhaps for Morris, too. When his order was ready, Russell paid the cashier. On his way out, he dropped another fifty cents into the *Chronicle* box, reached inside, grabbed the entire stack of papers, and tossed them into a dumpster in the parking lot. He hurried back to the room. Morris was still asleep.

"Phillip, wake up," he said, gently shaking him. "We've

got to get moving. My picture is on the front page of the paper. We need to get somewhere."

Up until that point, Morris claims, he was under the impression Russell had been paroled, and that he had always expected that Russell would find a way back to him—legally—by Friday the 13th. He now was furious, but sprang out of bed and began gathering his belongings. Between hurried mouthfuls of bacon and eggs, he made a suggestion.

"Maybe we should go to Biloxi. You've got a history in Florida, and they're going to be watching for you there. Biloxi is a transient sort of city. We can blend into the crowd. Plus, they've got casinos. We can have some fun while we're hiding out."

Russell was in no mood to argue. He also decided that even though they were on the run, they should travel in style. He made a call and before long a black limousine pulled up in front of the motel. Morris and Russell slid into the back seat. On the way to Biloxi, Mississippi, they watched *Pretty Woman* on the limo's VCR. But the driver's unusual behavior proved more interesting than the movie. "He acted like he was on crack, and he admitted to us that he was wanted [by the authorities]," says Russell. "In fact, when we arrived in Biloxi, he scored some dope while I bought us some food."

After they checked into a motel there, Russell went to

work on the phone to obtain some more money. He refuses to discuss who he called.

"I have about fourteen people who know me by another name," he says. "They helped out with the cash. I don't want to name them for obvious reasons. No one, including Phillip, knows who they are. I've always paid every single one of them back. I haven't burned those bridges. Basically, it was people who I dated in the past while I was married. They live everywhere."

Their cash replenished, the two men decided to enjoy Biloxi's casinos for a few days. When he wasn't at the gaming tables, Russell pored over classified ads in newspapers from all over the country looking for a job. Philadelphia offered the best prospects. Morris agreed to the destination. They would leave on an Amtrak train on Christmas Eve.

One evening before that, when he was returning from a stroll on the beach, Morris says, he saw Russell walking into an adult bookstore. Consumed with jealousy, Morris stormed into their motel room, bolted the door, and refused to let Russell back in.

"When Steve got back," he says, "I called the desk clerk and told them to call the police, that somebody I didn't know was trying to get into my room."

The police never arrived, and Morris finally allowed Russell in. At that point, Morris claims, he told Russell he was through with life on the run, and that he would be returning to Texas the following day. But Russell still had other ideas.

The next morning, Russell walked to a pay phone and called Helen Kemple, who now lived in Pennsylvania. He told her he was soon coming to Philadelphia. During the conversation, Kemple told Russell she heard another man's voice on the line.

"I thought this was odd since I was on a public telephone," says Russell. "I didn't tell her how we were getting to Philadelphia or where we were. Nor did she say that anyone from TDCJ had called her."

Russell hung up and returned to the room feeling paranoid, scenarios of his getting caught racing through his head. Somehow, TDCJ must have connected Helen to the money she had wired to Russell and they must have tapped her phone. Russell returned to the pay phone.

"I called her back to see if anyone had called her about us. She said they hadn't. But she did say that someone had called, and she heard noise on the answering machine."

Confused and concerned, Russell started walking back to the room. About a quarter-mile from the motel, he crossed right in front of three Biloxi police officers and a U.S. Marshal who were looking for him. They arrested him on the spot without incident.

While Russell was calling Helen the second time, Morris had headed for the casino. When he returned, his key wouldn't open the door, but he saw through a window that his suitcase and belongings were piled on the floor. Assuming Russell had abandoned him, he headed for the front desk to report that his key didn't work. As he entered the lobby, a police car pulled into the motel's driveway.

Two hours later, Russell and Morris sat side by side, handcuffed to a bench, awaiting transport back to Texas, courtesy of the state.

chapter thirteen

The Greatest Escape; The King is Dead, Long Live the King

In March 1998, 40-year-old Steven Russell checked into the Restful Acres Care Center, a place almost nobody wants to go. For starters, it's in Kenedy, a forlorn town southeast of San Antonio suffering from Wal-Mart syndrome. Once a thriving agricultural center, Kenedy as recently as the 1960s had boasted an impressive downtown for a small community. But the movie theater and shops on what once passed for a town square were by now boarded up, and the defunct grain elevator just south of what was once the central business district stood derelict, like a giant tombstone. The surrounding hills are dotted with purple-blooming prickly pear cactus and low to the ground mesquite trees with branches that look like arthritic fingers. Restful Acres is where Texas prisons send sick inmates to die.

Time and again during his career as a criminal and escape artist, Russell had relied on charm and guile to get him out of jams. But now things looked impossibly bleak. As he lay in his bed, the doctors and nurses treating him could do little more than watch helplessly as their patient withered away. Russell had been diagnosed by prison physicians as suffering through the final stages of AIDS.

After his most recent capture in Biloxi, Mississippi, and his return to the Texas prison system, Russell had lost drastic amounts of weight. He no longer walked without assistance. He did little more than lie in his infirmary bunk writing letters—many of them to Phillip Morris, who was now serving his own 20-year sentence for his alleged part in Russell's $800,000 embezzlement of North American Medical Management. But Russell continued to insist that Morris was innocent.

In addition to writing letters, Russell had also summoned enough energy to research an obscure division of the state's criminal-justice division known as the Texas Council on Offenders with Mental Impairments. Besides monitoring and administering the woefully limited mental health resources in Texas prisons, TCOMI officials are also in charge of a program called Special Needs Parole. Created by the Texas Legislature in the late 1980s, the program allows for the release of inmates, usually terminally ill ones, who require medical treatment the prisons cannot provide. It is a little known and seldom-used form of parole. And it was exactly what the doctor ordered for Russell. Although he had used this Jimmy Kemple-inspired scam before to win his release from federal prison in New Jersey, this time around Russell would take the plan to new heights. This time, he would outdo himself. This would be his most bodacious escape ever.

"In order to be successful with a Special Needs medical discharge," says Russell, who weighed about 200 pounds at the time of his arrest in Biloxi in December 1996, "I realized I would have to lose a considerable amount of weight. So I began to discipline myself to only eating half of what was served to me initially, and then one-quarter of what I was served after two weeks. I continued to monitor every single thing I ate until October 1997. By then my weight was down to 153 pounds. I looked like hell!"

But in addition to altering his physical appearance, to ensure that prison officials didn't suspect that his weight loss was just another one of his trademark ruses, Russell also needed to manipulate his medical files to corroborate his contention that he was indeed dying of AIDS. He decided to create a set of medical records that would show he had been infected with the HIV virus long before his sudden weight loss. At the prison library, he checked out every available book on the disease, looking for information that might not have been available during his tutelage from his old friend Dr. Kones.

"Opportunistic infections and low T-cell counts," he says, "were the keys." Enlisting the typing skills of an inmate who worked in the law library of the Telford Unit (one of the state prisons to which he had been assigned), Russell manufactured a new medical history for himself. When prison doctors from the University of Texas Medical Branch (UTMB) in Galveston, which contracts with the state to provide health care for inmates, later read Russell's bogus records, they swallowed them whole.

"I duplicated a typical lab report from UTMB showing a progressive decline in my T-cells, and enhanced the number of opportunistic infections I was afflicted with until I was eventually diagnosed with full-blown AIDS," he says. To get his fabricated records into his prison medical files, he simply dropped them into the prison's internal mail system. No member of the prison medical staff ever tested Russell's blood themselves.

To thwart any escape plan he might concoct, after his capture in Mississippi, corrections officials frequently relocated Russell to different prisons, four of them in a ten-month span. Russell used the transfers to his advantage. Each time he moved, his medical records were sent to his new location a few days later. At each new prison, Russell enlisted the help of cooperative inmates working in the infirmary to further update his charts.

"None of these guys knew what this fake information meant or what I was doing," he says. "This prevented me from being snitched on."

In October 1997, when he got transferred to the Stiles Unit just south of Beaumont, he took his plan to the next phase. He insisted on being relocated to a nursing home. Otherwise, he threatened he would refuse any treatment and die in prison. The bluff worked. Two weeks later the Texas State Board of Pardons and Paroles granted Russell a Special Needs Parole and plans were made to transport him to Restful Acres. At no point did prison medical personnel actually test Russell's blood themselves.

Ecstatic, Russell decided to celebrate, nearly shattering his scheme in the process.

Famished after ten months of dieting, he began to feast. His legs ached from inactivity, so he allowed himself to walk a little. He failed to realize that, just before a Special Needs inmate gets released, a doctor conducts a final exam. Russell's check-up indicated sudden improvement. His parole was yanked.

Not surprisingly, Russell's health again began to decline. This time he would neither speak nor get out of bed. He also became incontinent. He convinced prison doctors to prescribe hydrochlorothiazide to control his blood pressure, and doxepin to help him sleep. Russell hoarded the drugs, then took them all at once. For four days he slept almost constantly. Concerned guards informed medical personnel, and Russell was moved to the prison infirmary. His blood pressure hit rock bottom.

At the infirmary, Russell continued snoozing almost nonstop for two more days. Alarmed, the doctor in charge of the clinic, Dr. Mohammad Amir of UTMB, requested a Special Needs Parole, saving Russell the trouble of asking for one himself. Initially, the doctor suggested Russell be moved to the prison's main medical facility at the UT medical school in Galveston, but Russell strongly opposed this. He knew that at UTMB there would be too much supervision; it would be too much like prison. No, Russell told the doctor, he'd rather die in prison.

"So," he says, "they put a catheter in me and began the death watch."

Russell's apparent relapse caused Dr. Amir great concern. Again he contacted state officials about granting a Special Needs Parole, and transferring Russell to a facility where he could get the specialized treatment Dr. Amir was convinced he needed.

"HIV[-positive] since [19]90," wrote Dr. Amir on January 12, 1998, in a medical summary to the Board of Par-

dons and Parole. "In general condition [has] deteriorated over last four weeks with general weakness and
inability to speak." He had prescribed antibiotics and
antidiarrheal drugs, Amir reported, as well as "morphine
for pain control." Under the section labeled Final Diag-
nosis, Amir wrote: "End stage AIDS." The doctor pro-
jected that Russell had less than a month to live. Once
again, neither Amir nor anyone else with the prison
medical staff bothered to test Russell's blood for HIV.

During this same period, Russell was scheduled to face
an arraignment in a state district court in Huntsville, for
his escape from Estelle Unit in 1996 disguised as a doctor.
Once again, Amir rode to the rescue, informing the court
that the only way Russell could attend the hearing was on
a stretcher. Upon hearing this, the special prosecutor,
Latham Boone, had the escape indictment dismissed.

"Defendant is terminally ill and expected to die within
the month," Boone wrote on February 13, 1998. "Special
Needs Parole recommended, see attached. Parole plan
would allow defendant to die in a nursing home at families [sic] expense."

Eleven days later, Russell arrived at Restful Acres in an
ambulance. Immediately, he told the nursing home's
chief physician, Dr. Gary DeSiqueroa, that he wanted no
treatment whatsoever; he simply wanted to be left alone
to die.

Next, using telephones inside the home but taking care not to let any other ex-inmates convalescing there overhear him, Russell set up an account with a Houston answering service under the name of Dr. Adam Rios, the actual name of a prominent Houston physician who specializes in treating AIDS patients. As far back as 1985, Rios, a clinical immunologist at M. D. Anderson Hospital and Tumor Institute in Houston, had been involved in the development of experimental AIDS drugs and treatments. The doctor had once treated one of Russell's coworkers in the food industry. Russell made sure that anytime someone called the number, they were told they had reached Dr. Rios's answering service.

Again using phones inside the nursing home, he telephoned the facility's own Dr. DeSiqueroa. Posing as Dr. Rios, Russell told DeSiqueroa that he would like to perform experimental AIDS therapy on one of DeSiqueroa's patients, a Steven Russell. DeSiqueroa agreed, but informed "Rios" that they would need the Board of Pardon and Paroles to grant permission.

According to Russell, he then used the nursing home phone again, this time to call Victor Rodriguez, the executive director of the Board of Pardons and Paroles—a man who was quite familiar with Russell's track record as a con man and escape artist. Russell says that during the call he again posed as Dr. Rios and that Rodriguez bought the ruse completely.

Rodriguez, however did not return my phone calls, so there's no way to know if Russell's story is true. However, with Rodriguez's approval, TCOMI officials recommended that Russell's request to undergo experimental AIDS therapy be approved. According to state records, in early March, TCOMI program specialist Esther Herklotz sent a memorandum to the Texas Board of Pardons and Paroles suggesting Russell be allowed to travel to Houston for the care. "The releasee's family," she wrote, "will provide the transportation to and from the nursing home and Houston." Rodriguez initialled the document.

Russell was released from Restful Acres on March 13, 1998, not only a Friday the 13th but also Phillip Morris's 39th birthday. When Russell left, apparently no one at the nursing home took note that the person picking him up was not a relative. The week before, Russell had called a local car lot and asked a salesman to bring a 1991 Hyundai by the nursing home for his inspection. He told the staff at the home that he wanted to buy a car for his mother so that she could come visit him. Using money that he still had stashed away in a personal bank account, Russell bought the car for $3,200 and told the dealer to hold it back on his lot until March 13. On the day of his release, Russell arranged to be fetched from the home by taxi.

While doing time at the Stiles Unit, Russell had struck up a friendship with an inmate whose stepfather, Don Dobbins, drove a cab in San Antonio. In a letter, the inmate had told Dobbins that his friend Steven Russell might someday need a favor. That day turned out to be March 13.

"He worked for Yellow Cab, and I paid him two hundred dollars to pick me up under the guise that he was taking me to Houston for medical treatment," Russell says.

Instead, Russell instructed Dobbins to drive him to the car dealership, where he claimed his Hyundai and immediately set out for Houston. Shortly thereafter, Russell claims he purchased a copy of the Harris County seal from an office supply store. He then purchased some surgical scrubs and, once again posing as a doctor, obtained some blank death certificates from a funeral home. A few days later, Restful Acres and Russell's parole officer received the official-looking documents informing that Russell was dead. And once Steven Russell was dead, he was off and running, and in search of his reason for living: Phillip Morris.

In the aftermath of his and Russell's capture in Biloxi, and their return to Houston, Phillip Morris had stood trial and been found guilty of helping Russell steal the $800,000 from North American Medical Management. For his participation in the embezzlement, Morris received a 20-year sentence in the Texas prison system. From that point on, in addition to his own freedom, Russell became obsessed with finding a way of clearing Morris's name, and with getting Morris out of jail so they could reunite.

"I believed that with the proper representation, Phillip could get a reversal based on legally insufficient evidence, which should have resulted in an acquittal," says Russell, the would-be lawyer. "I also thought that with me dead, we could live together without the authorities looking for either of us."

The day after leaving Restful Acres, Russell rented an unfurnished apartment in Galveston, where he intended to keep a low profile and seek an out-of-state job. He then drove back north on Interstate 45 to Gallery Furniture, located off the freeway just north of downtown Houston.

Since going into business in the mid-1970s, Gallery's owner, Jim "Mattress Mac" MacInvale, had become one of Houston's best-known and wealthiest men. He's famous for TV commercials in which he screams maniacally at the camera about the quality of his goods and the bargains to be had in his store.

"Gallery Furniture really will SAVE...YOU...MONEY!" he says while jumping into the air and waving a fistful of dollars. Should any potential customers shudder at the thought of their neighbors finding out that they've shopped at Gallery, one of Mac's commercials points out that his company can deliver furniture to a buyer's home in unmarked trucks, sort of in the spirit of mail-order pornography arriving in a plain brown wrapper.

Russell had dressed casually that Saturday afternoon—T-shirt, shorts, loafers with no socks—but as he entered the store, he conspicuously flashed the gold Rolex on his right wrist which he had picked up after again getting a loan from a friend in Florida. Sensing a sell, a Gallery salesman took the bait.

"How you doing today, sir?" he asked. "I'm Chili Richardson. Can I help you find what you're looking for today?"

"I sure hope so, Chili," said Russell. "I'm Art Sandler. I've just been transferred from Florida. Got promoted to president of the local Monsanto operation. But they didn't give me time to move any of my stuff. I rented this temporary apartment in Galveston this morning, but it's an unfurnished place. I was hoping you could set me up—make it livable until I find a house and have my stuff moved here."

"You've come to the right place," said Richardson.

For the next hour or so, they toured the Gallery showrooms. Along the way, Russell selected $3,000 worth of furniture, and he told Richardson he wanted to pay on Gallery's in-house credit plan.

"No problem," the salesman said. "I'll just need to see some identification so I can run a credit check."

"I was afraid you were going to say that," said Russell. "You're not going to believe this, but somebody stole my new BMW 750 last night out of the motel parking lot. My wallet and all my personal checks were in the glove compartment."

This seemed like a stretch, and Richardson was a bit suspicious. So Russell casually dropped the name of Mattress Mac and Mac's brother-in-law.

"Me and him and Mac and my boss at Monsanto used to play golf together," he lied.

That seemed strange to Richardson, too. MacInvale doesn't golf. Despite his misgivings, however, Richardson handed Russell a credit application form. On the questionnaire, Russell claimed that he earned $10,000 a month. After a credit check, Russell/Sandler was somehow approved for credit, but only up to $2,500. Since the furniture he had selected cost $3,000, Richardson told him he would have to pay the balance in cash. Russell had none.

"I thought that was strange, too," Richardson would say later. "Because a guy making $10,000 a month ought to have a pocket full of money."

But Russell convinced Richardson to confer with his bosses. Amazingly, the store's brass decided to accept

Russell's non-personalized check, put the rest of the tab on credit, and deliver the furniture to Galveston.

Two days later, Russell called the Virginia Department of Vital Statistics, and asked the clerk he spoke with to FedEx him a copy of the birth certificate of Art Sandler, the owner of Sandler Foods who had purchased the Russell family produce business. Posing as an attorney, he called Morris at the Estelle Unit. He told a nervous Morris that he had faked his own death, that he loved him, and that he would see him soon. Next, he bought a computer, set up an answering-service account in the name of Monsanto, reviewed help-wanted ads in the *Wall Street Journal*, and began searching for an attorney to handle Morris's appeal.

On Tuesday, after receiving a copy of Sandler's birth certificate, Russell caught a Southwest Airlines flight from Houston to Oklahoma City. There, he applied for an Oklahoma driver's license as Art Sandler.

"Why Oklahoma?" he asks rhetorically. "Because [the Oklahoma driver's license bureau] did not have digital photography or require fingerprints. States that take laser prints run those prints through NCIC to make sure there are no warrants on file, and to make sure that multiple driver's licenses from other states are not already in existence. Texas fingerprints! They are also on-line with

Social Security to make sure that multiple licenses aren't issued, and dead people aren't resurrected."

He flew back to Houston the same day. The next morning, again posing as an attorney, he attempted to contact Morris by phone at the Estelle Unit, but learned Morris had been transferred to Dallas County Jail, to testify in the trial of his former lover, Mel, in connection with a 1983 theft indictment. Russell had not foreseen this. The lawyers he had contacted about representing Morris now wanted $25,000 for the appeal and another $25,000 for handling the Dallas court appearance.

That same week, Russell claims he convinced someone at the state bar association that he was an attorney named Gene Lewis, that he had lost his bar card, and that he needed a replacement sent immediately. Desperate to see Morris as soon as possible, he flew to Austin and picked up the card in person. (There apparently is a real Texas attorney named Gene Lewis, but he knew nothing of Russell's scheme.) On Friday morning Russell flew to Dallas, and immediately went to the county jail, posing as Lewis. Russell was already sitting in the visitation booth when a guard brought in Morris, wearing a white jump suit.

"Damn, it's good to see you," said Morris. "You look great. How do I look?"

"Great!" replied Russell. "Can you believe I'm out?"

"Yes, actually I can. When it comes to you, I'll believe just about anything. When they transported me up here, I expected to see you in a guard uniform on the bus."

"I wish. If that were the case, we wouldn't be looking at each other through this Plexiglas right now."

"How did you get me transferred here?" asked Morris.

"I didn't. The Dallas district attorney's office did. There's some sort of outstanding indictment and theft charge from 1983 when you and Mel were together."

"Damn. I wonder why that's never come up before. I'm not guilty of that bullshit. Mel worked at this landscaping and lighting company, and was billing them from dummy companies he set up that never did any work. But I wasn't involved in it."

"Yeah, I remember you telling me that. I guess it's sort of like what happened to you with me. Anyway, I'm trying to get all this shit resolved. Each case is going to cost $25,000. But I think I can get this Dallas charge dismissed for lack of a speedy trial."

Russell filled Morris in on the details of his recent death. They both had a laugh, then fell silent.

"I'm really sorry I got you into this mess, Phillip," Russell said solemnly. "Do you want me to get you out on early parole?"

"You mean escape?" Morris asked nervously.

"Yes."

"No, honey. I can't do that. I haven't done anything wrong. Escaping would only make me look guilty. I'm still upset with you for tricking me into jumping bond and running off to Biloxi. Besides, it's harder for two to hide than one."

"Okay then, I've got another idea," said Russell, refusing to give up. "What if I dress up like a TDCJ major, and come back here at night with an order from a Harris County court to get you a medical exam at one of the TDCJ units? We could just leave for a few hours, and then come back."

"I like that idea. I sure would love to get out of here for a few hours. But I can't do it."

"Okay, then I've got another idea I want to run past you."

He flashed Morris his Art Sandler license.

"How in the world did you get that?" asked Morris. "Never mind. I'm sorry I asked."

"I'm going to go down to NationsBank and borrow $75,000 in Art's name. It's going to take $50,000 to get you out of jail. This would cover that, and there would be some left over."

"Don't you think that's a little risky?" Morris countered. "Why don't you just get a job? You could make $2,000 a week as a CFO. I don't want to lose you again to these people."

"Because it will take a fucking year to come up with

$50,000," said Russell, getting somewhat irritated at Morris's reservations. "Your appeal brief is due damn soon. I talked to the lawyer that's been appointed to represent you. He's a goddamn idiot."

"He hasn't answered any of my letters," said Morris. "He's never even come to see me."

"I spoke with him in the phone yesterday. I'm worried that he's going to fuck up your appeal. He sounds like a real lazy ass."

"Aren't they all?"

"Are you sure you just don't want your prince to come and rescue you from this dump?" asked Russell.

"Yes, I do. But I want to get out of here the right way."

"Okay," said Russell dejectedly. "Look, why don't we take a break for a while? I'm going to go get something to eat. After lunch, I'll come back and we can talk some more, and decide what to do."

"I sure do love you," said Morris.

"I love you, too," said Russell.

In truth, Russell had made up his mind before setting foot in the jail. On the flight to Dallas, he had phoned Nations-Bank to request a $75,000 loan in Art Sandler's name. After leaving the jail, he headed straight for the bank.

Unfortunately for Russell, NationsBank personnel proved to be a bit sharper than he'd expected. While he sat in the bank lobby waiting for the loan to get approved, bank officers notified their security team that Russell might not be who he said he was. Within a few minutes, security guards whisked him into a conference room. The chief security officer confiscated Russell's fake Monsanto ID card and his Oklahoma license. He also called the FBI, which dispatched an agent.

Before the FBI arrived, Russell developed chest pains, or at least he claimed he did. An ambulance transported him to Baylor Medical Center's emergency room.

When Russell tried to leave, some police officers stopped him, and told him he was being held under investigative detention. One of them took Russell's wallet, which contained the card identifying him as Gene Lewis. They did not take Russell's cell phone.

"After they transferred me to a room, I called the Baylor dispatcher [on an in-house phone]," he says. "I identified myself as Special Agent Thomas of the FBI, and told her to transfer me to the watch officer. A lieutenant answered, and I re-identified myself, and I told him that they didn't need to detain the suspect any longer."

Shortly after the phone call, the Baylor security officer who had confiscated Russell's wallet returned it to him, and told him he was free to leave.

"I exited the building, and hauled ass across the parking lot," he says. "You should have seen me run. You would have thought they were shooting at me."

After clearing the hospital campus, Russell took a cab to downtown Dallas, bought a green jogging outfit at Neiman-Marcus, and wore it out of the store. He then returned to the county jail to brief Morris on the day's developments. Since Russell had been gone some four hours longer than they'd planned, and was now wearing green warm-ups, Morris had an inkling that something had gone wrong.

"What happened?" he asked in a tone that indicated he was not pleased.

"I went to the bank and almost ended up getting myself put in a cell next you, that's what happened."

"Oh, shit," said Morris, lighting the first of a continuous sequence of Marlboro Lights. Russell recounted the afternoon's events, then asked, "What do you think I should do?"

"It's a little late to be asking me what you ought to do," Morris shot back.

"Yeah, I know," Russell confessed. "I guess I'll go back to Galveston and get my stuff."

"Honey, where do you think up all this shit?" Morris asked. "I'm going to be worried sick until I know you've gotten out of there."

"I'll load up the car, drive back up here, and come see

you as soon as I get back to Dallas," said Russell. "They don't have any specific times for lawyer visits. They told me I could visit you anytime."

"Okay, but I'll be on pins and needles until you get back. Remember, I love you."

"I love you, too, babe. It'll be okay."

But Russell no longer felt as confident as he tried to sound. Before boarding his plane back to Houston, he tried to determine just how vigorously he was being pursued. Around seven o'clock that Friday evening, he called the local FBI office and identified himself as a special agent from Washington, D.C. "I understand that Agent Tierney in your office has been assigned to that possible case of bank fraud over at NationsBank there in Dallas this afternoon," he said.

"Yes, sir, that's correct," said the voice on the other end.

"Can I speak with him please?" asked Russell.

"I'm sorry, sir, he's already left for the day."

"That's okay. I'll just call him Monday."

"I'm sorry. Agent Tierney is scheduled to be on the firing range Monday. He won't be back in the office until Tuesday morning."

Russell now knew he had at least three days of relative freedom. He flew back to Houston and drove to his apartment in Galveston. Russell knew it was just a matter of time before the feds realized it had been him posing as

Art Sandler at the bank. Since he had used Sandler's name for the credit check at the apartment complex, he feared the FBI might already be looking for him there. He needed to get back to the apartment and gather up as much stuff as he could—especially the computer—before they came knocking.

In Galveston, he staked out his apartment for an hour before entering. Once inside, he packed up everything he needed and everything that could be traced back to him, and stashed it in his car. The next morning he drove back to Dallas.

Following his narrow escapes at NationsBank and Baylor Medical Center the day before, Russell was primarily concerned about the FBI. But as it turned out, they weren't the only ones following his trail. Russell's interest in obtaining an ID card in Gene Lewis's name had triggered alarms at the state bar office. Something about his request did not ring true. Concerned that he might be an impostor, bar officials decided to distribute a copy of Russell's photograph, which he had had taken for the ID card, to law enforcement agencies across Texas.

One of those agencies was the Gulf Coast Violent Offenders Task Force, which is based in Houston and comprised of officers from several different agencies in the state. One of those officers was Terry Cobbs, an official with the TDCJ who had helped bring Russell back from Biloxi after his December 1996 escape. Cobbs is a dedicated, sharp-minded man with a quick wit. His large frame and shaved head make him physically intimidating, a useful trait for a man who specializes in tracking fugitives. He was a member of the team that captured the so-called Texas Seven, a murderous group of inmates who escaped from a south Texas jail in December 2000.

On a Monday morning in March 1998 when Cobbs reported to work at the task force's headquarters, what he saw astonished him. There, pinned to the squad room's bulletin board, was a photograph of Steven Russell, accompanied by a note from the state bar requesting information about the mystery lawyer.

"This can't be right," said Cobbs, staring at the photo. "This is Steven Russell, and he's in jail. I put him in jail for 45 years. This is impossible."

Cobbs began running checks. He logged on to his computer, and was soon shocked to learn that Russell had received Special Needs Parole and gotten transferred from a state prison to a nursing home. Growing more alarmed and angry by the second, he called Russell's parole officer in Seguin, Texas, not far from the nursing home in Kenedy.

"I'm calling about one of your clients, Steven Russell," Cobbs said. "He has a history of escape, and I'm afraid he may be up to something."

"He's not up to anything," the officer said. "He's dead. I've got a copy of the death certificate right here."

Cobbs knew better, and he was now furious. Aware of Russell's obsession with Phillip Morris, he checked on Morris's whereabouts and learned of his recent transfer to Dallas County Jail. He then called the jail to warn officials there to keep an eye on Morris and anyone who visited him. Visitation records revealed that, in fact, a lawyer named Gene Lewis had come to see Morris at least three times in recent days. Cobbs and Dallas County deputies laid their trap and waited for Russell to return. He did not.

A day or two later, with the help of the FBI, Cobbs located Russell's apartment in Galveston. Once again, Russell was already gone. The fugitive hunter remained one step behind his prey.

After clearing out his Galveston apartment that Friday night, Russell had immediately driven back to Dallas. True to his word, he returned to the county jail around 5:00 A.M. for a brief visit with Morris before hitting the road. After that, he couldn't risk returning to the jail again. To maintain contact with Morris, Russell decided to set up a system through which they could still communicate by telephone. That afternoon, he set up yet another account at an answering service, and arranged for the operators to answer calls as if their client was a law firm.

"I set it up so that Phillip could call at specified times, and they would accept the collect charge from the jail," he says. "Then the two of us could be conferenced in together. I did this because after they found out who I was—and I was sure they would—I wouldn't be able to call him directly, much less go see him."

Russell assumed, correctly, that the FBI would identify him through fingerprints he had left at Baylor Medical Center. He didn't know that Cobbs was on to him as well.

That same afternoon, Russell left Dallas and drove without incident to Sunrise, Florida, a suburb of Fort Lauderdale. There he rented living quarters at the Sawgrass Apartments under the name Edward Wallace Wolcott Jr., an attorney who had once represented him in Virginia. He obtained a Florida driver's license in the same name, and used Wolcott's credit to buy a computer and a fax machine.

Each day, playing it safe, Russell drove to Boca Raton to call Morris by way of the answering service. Morris warned him that jail guards were watching him closely and monitoring the numbers he called. To keep them guessing, he made 30 to 60 calls a day to a variety of numbers.

On April 26, Russell called the Dallas County Jail, himself, not to speak with Morris, but with one of the jailers. Russell identified himself as a deputy with the Dallas County sheriff.

"Afternoon, deputy," the jailer said. "What can I do for you?"

"I'm out looking for this Steven Russell character. You know, that guy that passed himself off as an attorney last week at the jail so he could visit his little boyfriend. I'm just checking to make sure he hasn't been back—and that the boyfriend, Phillip Clark Morris, is still where he's supposed to be."

"Oh yeah, he's here all right," said the jailer. "Matter of fact, we've got a sting operation set up. We're just sitting here waiting for his lawyer to come back. And then we'll grab him."

"Just double-checking," said Russell. "Keep up the good work!"

As all of this transpired, Russell remained obsessed with getting enough money to hire an attorney who could get Morris out of prison. As a first step, he claims, he contacted friends in Florida who knew him by a different name, and gathered enough money from them to set up an account in Wolcott's name at First Union Bank. He also arranged for a $9,000 credit line for overdraft protection. That left him $41,000 short of the amount he needed. He contacted the bank again to request a $50,000 loan. He consulted with a plastic surgeon about changing the appearance of his lips, eyes and nose. The surgeries would cost $10,000, which he arranged to pay on credit through Jayhawk Financing. While trying to arrange the loan and the surgery, Russell worked on a fallback plan. In case he didn't get the loan, he considered the possibility of using his computer to simulate life insurance policies, then sell them to viatical companies under the pretense that he was dying from AIDS. On his computer, he re-chronicled the progression of James Kemple's battle with the disease. He consulted over the phone with infectious disease specialists about recent advancements in AIDS treatment. And he arranged for an answering service to field his calls under the name DuPont Biotechnology.

All this time, Cobbs and other officers were closing in.

Three weeks earlier, on April 5, 1998, Palm Sunday, Cobbs contacted Special Agent Richard Dees of the Florida Department of Law Enforcement. Cobbs told Dees that from analyzing Morris's phone records, and from Russell's previous masquerade at Gallery Furniture as an official with DuPont, he had reason to believe his prey might have landed in southern Florida. "Cobbs knew about the viatical angle from reading a story about me in the *Houston Press*," says Russell. "So he started calling this viatical guy in Florida to see if anyone had tried to sell him a new policy. Turns out it was one of the guys I had contacted, and he told Cobbs about DuPont. Right then, Cobbs knew he was on the right track."

Dees agreed to join the hunt. By Tuesday he had honed in on Sunrise and the Sawgrass Apartments; Russell thinks the security guard at the complex may have run a check on his Texas license plates. In any case, Dees and his partner arrived in separate unmarked cars at the pink stucco buildings. As soon as he got there, Dees saw a man fitting Russell's description.

Russell went inside and fixed himself dinner. After eating, he planned to drive to a drugstore to fill a prescription for antibiotics in anticipation of the cosmetic surgery. Before he could get to his car, Dees had a 9-millimeter up against his head.

"Cobbs did great detective work," Russell says admiringly. "I'll give him that." But in the very next breath, he seems to set the stage for a rematch. "If they hadn't had Phillip, they never would have caught me. That's the last time Cobbs will ever get to make a fool out of me."

When Steven Russell returned to Texas in April 1998, once again in the custody of fugitive-tracking law officers, the promised media interviews or photo opportunities were abrubtly canceled without explanation. Of course, no explanation was needed. This time Russell had made state prison officials look foolish—never a good thing, but especially not when their boss, Governor George W. Bush, was preparing to run for president.

"[Russell] is going to be so far behind bars, he's going to have to have his sunshine shipped in by Federal Express," a TDCJ public affairs officer told reporters.

Early, the TDCJ public affairs office had told the media that the state plane carrying Russell back from Florida would be landing at Houston's Bush Intercontinental Airport, and that there would be a perp walk and an opportunity for questions. Instead, Russell's flight bypassed Houston entirely, taking him directly to the Michael Unit, one of several prisons located near the rural east Texas city of Palestine.

Upon his return, the new TDCJ special prosecutor, Kelly Weeks, refiled charges against Russell for his 1996 escape from the Estelle Unit, in which he dyed his prison uniform green and posed as a doctor. (Weeks had taken over for Latham Boone, the special prosecutor who had signed off on Russell's request for a Special Needs Parole.)

In August 2000, a Huntsville, Texas, jury took only thirty minutes to find Russell guilty of escape. During the punishment phase of the trial, Weeks asked the jurors to sentence Russell under the state's habitual criminal statute, which allows three-time felons to be confined to prison for life regardless of the seriousness or violence level of their offenses.

"[Russell] isn't violent, but he hurts people," Weeks told the jury. She did not, however, mention that one of Russell's victims, former NAMM executive Don Holmquist, is her brother-in-law.

"[Russell has] ruined people's lives by thievery. And that can be just as bad as physically hurting them," Weeks continued. "Make sure he never sees the light of these streets and never hurts another person again. And make sure it sends a message that Terry Cobbs doesn't have to go out and look for him [again]. And make sure that innocent people aren't hurt again. Send him a message."

Which is exactly what the jury did. In addition to his 45-year sentence for the NAMM embezzlement, Russell is also serving a life sentence for the crime of escape. He will be eligible for parole in approximately sixty years.

Since his most recent capture, Russell has resided at the Michael Unit, a cluster of gray concrete slab buildings surrounded by razor-wire fences. Because of his history, he is housed in administrative segregation—solitary confinement—and confined to a six-by-seven-foot cell with a solid steel door with a padlock. He is allowed out of his cell for one hour each day. Each time, he is strip-searched. Twice each week, he is moved to a new cell. During each move, guards search his belongings.

Each day at 3:00 A.M. Russell gets up for breakfast. After an hour of meditation, he exercises in his cell for two-and-a-half to three hours.

"What I do is step up and down off of my bed," he says of his version of box aerobics. "The bed is two feet off the floor, so you get a good cardio workout."

He alternates sit-ups with push-ups every other day. He's up to 700 of the former and 300 of the latter. This regimen has helped him reduce his body weight—which had gone back up to about 225 pounds—to 150, and his waist from 44 inches to 32. One day he was summoned to the warden's office. Someone had brought his sudden interest in physical fitness to the warden's attention.

"He called me in and wanted to know what I was up to," he says, chuckling.

Russell showers sometime between seven and eight-thirty in the morning. Then he writes letters, reads mail, and listens to the radio—usually the National Public Radio station in Dallas or a soft rock station in Tyler. When friends and relatives send books, he reads each day. Mysteries and suspense novels are his favorites. He subscribes to *USA Today*, and to *The Wall Street Journal* to keep up with the stock market.

Lunch falls between 11:00 and noon, dinner between three and four. Mail call is at seven. Thirty minutes later, clean prison uniforms are issued. After that, he tries to sleep. As he dozes off, he either listens to the radio or wears earplugs to filter out the sounds other inmates.

Russell's mail often comes to him delayed and censored, especially letters from Phillip Morris, who writes from the Hughes Unit, a prison near Gatesville, southwest of Waco in central Texas. Despite the censorship, Russell says he and Morris communicate between the lines.

"Writing to each other has been a real challenge," he says. "We put extra meaning into everything we write, and the average person doesn't have a clue as to what we're talking about. We basically read each other's minds. We use codes and phrases and talk in circles. Every word has a meaning that only the other would understand. The same was true when we could see each other or talk to each other. I attribute all of this to our intense ability to be intimate, even though we are incarcerated and separate."

Russell also gets mail from his ex-wife, Debbie, and his daughter, Stephanie. In a letter on file at the Harris County DA's office, Debbie indicated that she and Russell have remained close despite their divorce, his incarceration, and his homosexuality.

"Just a note to let you know that Stephanie and I appreciate all you've tried to do to make our lives comfortable," she wrote. "None of us have had the easiest, best road, but we've had a closeness that few can understand."

If Russell has to leave the prison for any reason—like an optometrist appointment or a court appearance—a TDCJ internal affairs officer follows his bus.

"Some day they will eventually put me on a handtruck and strap me down like Hannibal Lecter," he says with a laugh.

But Russell also continues to think obsessively about Phillip Morris. He still hopes to find the attorney who will get Morris paroled. Indeed, during the time I worked on this book, Morris occupied the core of most of Russell's conversations with me, and letters to me. He also admits that his feelings for Morris have sometimes led to bad decisions.

"I believe I have two minds," he says. "One is emotional and the other is rational. Usually there is a balance between them. But when it comes to Phillip, my heart emotions can control me and overwhelm my instinct for survival.

"These days, I try to resist the desire for short-term fixes to long-term problems. I can't begin to give Phillip enough credit for helping me see through many of my weaknesses. He is so helpful to me, even from another unit. One of the biggest mistakes TDCJ made was trying to keep me away from Phillip. He is, like Jimmy was, the only fucking person I will listen to. No one else understands my psyche."

But while Russell insists that he and Morris will somehow reunite and spend the rest of their lives together in bliss, Morris seems somewhat ambivalent about the subject.

"I've talked to [Russell] about this," Morris says. "Right now I don't know. I can't answer that right now. My plan [after getting out] right now is to be close to my family. I want to go see my dad [in Arkansas]. My dad doesn't have a whole lot of time left, and I want to be there."

Of course, by downplaying his desire to eventually hook up with Russell, Morris could very well be playing to the parole board, speaking the words he hopes will increase his chances of convincing the board members to grant him an early release.

Russell, of course, doesn't talk directly about another potential "early release" of his own, though he is clearly intrigued by the topic. It's part of the cat-and-mouse game with prison officials that he loves. Almost as much as the freedom, it's the competition, the plotting, and the hunt that excites him. When he talks about his past triumphs, his eyes sparkle and dance—even behind a Plexiglas barrier.

"I live by the fact that you must never confuse the faith that you will prevail in the end—which you can never afford to lose—with the need for the discipline to confront the most brutal facts of your current reality," he says.

"That's why my life sentence or my 45-year sentence don't affect me or cause me to see my situation as hopeless. There have been times in the past that I have allowed hopelessness to control me. The mistakes I made when I've been captured were all tied to emotion instead of the brain God gave me. That won't happen again. The cops don't understand that I escape when I make up my mind to escape."

In Russell's opinion, there's little his keepers can do to stop him. He's engaged in a battle of wits with a prison staff he views as woefully underequipped. He has them exactly where he wants them. Again.

acknowledgments

Thanks to Lisa Chase of the Editor's Room and to Peter Borland for their edits that make me look smarter than I am. Thanks also to my personal editor-for-life, Lisa Gray, and to Bonnie Gangelhoff, my personal life editor, for their edits, suggestions, and threats. Also thanks to Jonathan Burnham and JillEllyn Riley of Miramax Books for giving me a shot. Thanks also to Marti Blumenthal of Writers and Artists Agency. And special thanks to Mark Schone and to the brilliant and handsome Peter Steinberg of JCA Literary Agency for making it all happen.

LaVergne, TN USA
15 February 2011
216648LV00004B/12/A